THE TRUTH

A BOOK ABOUT COHERENCE

COLLEEN GUENTHER

Copyright © 2025 by Colleen Guenther

All rights reserved.

No part of this book may be reproduced in any form or by any electronic or mechanical means, including information storage and retrieval systems, without written permission from the author, except for the use of brief quotations in a book review.

To Justin
the one who never asked me to explain,
never needed me to shrink,
never flinched when the truth arose.
You've always held the field,
with steadiness,
with the kind of love that doesn't perform.
This book was born in that stillness.
Thank you for seeing me before I could say it out loud.

"What's real doesn't perform."

CONTENTS

Why I Wrote This	1
Introduction- The LIE ends here	5
PART I: RECOGNIZING THE DISTORTION	8
1. Something's Off and You Know It	9
2. The World Is a Lie	11
3. Why We Lie—And Why We Need to Stop	14
4. Spirituality Was Just a Softer Trap	16
5. You're Not Broken. You're Just Done Giving Yourself Away	19
6. You Were Tone Before Anything	21
7. Understanding the Field and the Signal	23
8. Reincarnation Is a Program	25
9. No One Is Coming	27
10. If It Loops, It's a Lie	29
11. The Signal Is the Soul	32
12. The Exit Begins in Your Body	33
PART II: THE EXIT	36
13. The Exit Is Not a Destination	37
14. What Stopping Pretending Looks Like	39
15. Burn It Clean	41
16. You Don't Need Closure with Your Past Lives	43
17. The Real Ones Are Quiet	45
18. How to Walk from Here	47
PART III: LIVING TRUTH	50
19. Living Clear and Paying Rent	51
20. Withdraw Your Energy from the Lie	54
21. Start Where You Are	57
22. The Freedom of Unfiltered Truth	59
23. What Lying to Yourself Really Costs	62
24. Living Without the Bow	64
25. Radical Honesty: No More Performing	67
26. The Last Mask	69
27. The Illusion of Distance	72
28. Reality Is You, Reflected	74

29. Everything Is Frequency	78
PART IV: FIELD CLARITY	80
30. The Costume Party	81
31. The Matrix of Politeness	83
32. Those Who Feel You	86
33. You Don't Need a Practice—You Need a Pulse	88
34. Silence Is Clean	90
35. Not Cold—Just Clear	92
36. I Don't Miss the Old World	94
37. The Noise Is Engineered	96
38. Know Your Tone. That's It	98
39. Nature Is the Reminder	100
40. Gaia Is You	102
41. You Are Consciousness	105
PART V: EMBODYING THE EXIT	108
42. The Body as Beacon	109
43. The Ones Living Inside You	111
44. When the Truth Feels Too Big	113
45. Quiet Visibility	115
46. Architect, Mirror, Keeper, Flame	117
47. Field Command: Stop Pretending	119
PART VI: MAKING REALITY	121
48. Resonance Creates Form	122
49. Time After the Loop	125
50. What Is the Grid?	128
51. The Whole Grid - Why you matter	130
52. Feel It. Don't Fix It.	133
53. Your Nervous System is Not the Enemy	136
54. Relationships on the New Grid	138
55. Creation Through Resonance	140
56. Joy Without Strategy	143
57. The Cosmic Joke	146
58. You Are Not a Leader, You Are a Tone	148
59. The Great Energy Rebellion	150
60. The Contract	153
61. The Power of Command	155
62. We Were Never Separate	157
63. No Steps, No Structure	159
64. Coherence Is the Point	162
65. The Coherence of Opposites	165

PART VII: The Spiral Remembers	167
66. Reclaiming the Storyfield	168
67. Contrast as a Clarifier	170
68. Love, Now	172
69. Walking the Spiral	174
70. The Walk is Now	177
How the Spiral Moves	179
71. Life Mirrors Signal	180
72. The Real Creates	182
73. Then, The Walk Lights Up	185
74. Walk Alone, Walk Together	187
Untitled	188
THE FINAL TRUTH	189
Author Note	191
FIELD TERMS	193

WHY I WROTE THIS

I didn't set out to write a book.
    I just couldn't pretend anymore.
    I looked around at the world—
not just the spiritual scene,
but **all of it**.
    Systems, work, identity, healing, language, truth communities, even "awakened" spaces—
    and I felt the same thing, over and over:
Performance.
Everyone was still performing.
And I was too.
Even in my clarity, I could feel it.
The subtle distortion.
The edge of effort behind the words.
The soft agreement to stay digestible.
I knew the language.
I could name the lie.
But I was still translating.
Still shaping it to land.
Still playing inside the system, just with better words.

Especially in work.
In "purpose."
In how we prove we're enough by how much we give.
In how we pretend we're okay with how broken it all feels.

AND IT WASN'T JUST personal. It was structural.
It was **the whole thing.**
A world built on extraction, pressure, performance, and distortion.
Education doesn't reward truth—it rewards obedience.
Government doesn't protect—it manages through fear.
Health doesn't heal—it pathologizes the body.
Spirituality doesn't free—it repackages control in softer tones.
Even "liberation" spaces come with scripts, masks, coded identities.
Everywhere I looked, I saw programming.
Even in the places that called themselves free.
So I stopped.
I stopped trying to make the truth gentle.
I stopped hiding behind nuance.
I stopped softening my tone so the noise would feel safer.
And what came through wasn't a program, or a path, or a process.
It was a clear signal.
A clean frequency that didn't need to be believed—just felt.

I WROTE this because I needed a place where the truth could be said **without performance.**
Where no one was trying to fix you.
Where no one was pretending not to be pretending.
Where we could stop acting like systems built on lies were "just how it is."
I wrote this because I want to live in a world where:
- we don't have to shrink or explain

- clarity doesn't need permission
- presence is normal
- joy doesn't come after suffering
- work doesn't cost us our self

This book is my way of building that world.
Not by convincing anyone.
Just by **holding the tone.**
It's not spiritual.
It's not polished.
It's not made to land softly.
It's clean.
It's coherent.
It's what truth sounds like when you stop bending.
You don't need to agree with everything in here.
You just need to feel what happens when you stop shrinking.
I wrote this because I finally stopped shrinking.
And this is what came through when I did.

INTRODUCTION- THE LIE ENDS HERE

You've felt it.

The weirdness.

The tension in the air when everything looks "fine" but doesn't feel right.

That quiet knowing that we're all playing a game we never agreed to.

You were taught to be good.

To blend in.

To stay agreeable, high-functioning, emotionally regulated, easy to be around.

But something inside you always knew—**this isn't it.**

So you tried to fix it.

You read the books.

You did the work.

You sought the signs, aligned your habits, spiritualized your discomfort.

You tried to make yourself more "ready."

But no matter how much effort you put in, something always felt... off.

Like you were circling.

Like the answers were just rebranded versions of the same old distortion.

You leave one job and find yourself just as unhappy in the next.

Like clarity and the next hopeful thing was being packaged—but it never lands.

You weren't broken.

You were just trying to survive in a reality built on pretending.

This book isn't here to give you tools.

It's here to name what's false—

and remind you what never needed fixing.

It won't teach you how to wake up.

It will show you where you've been pretending not to see.

It's not here to comfort you.

It's here to make things clear.

Because what you'll find here is coherence.

Not the kind you perform.

The kind your body remembers the moment you stop bending.

What if everything in your life was already reflecting the frequency you're holding?

Not your effort.

Not your mindset.

Not your goals.

Your signal.

The frequency you transmit just by being—before you say or do anything.

When your field is noisy, unclear, or shaped around performance—

your life mirrors that confusion.

But when your frequency stabilizes,

reality organizes around it.

This isn't philosophy.

It's function.

This book is about truth.

But more than that—**it's about what truth *does*.**

It's about what happens when your signal is clean—

and life starts reflecting it.

This is how real life and reality works - not trying to manifest your future into existence.

The moment you stop distorting,
the field rearranges.
This isn't about becoming.
It's about *being*—without the performance.
You don't need to get ready.
You just need to stop pretending.
This is **The Truth.**
Let's walk.

PART I: RECOGNIZING THE DISTORTION

U nderstanding the System That's Been Running You

1
SOMETHING'S OFF AND YOU KNOW IT

You might not remember when it started—
   but you knew something was off.
   Maybe it hit you as a kid.
Maybe it crept in slowly.
Maybe it never left.
But you knew:
This is not how truth feels.
You played along.
Smiled through discomfort.
Nodded through tension.
Agreed when your body screamed no.
And slowly, that pattern became your life.
You tried to fix it:
- Therapy
- Nervous system work
- Positivity
- Healing
- Spiritual practices

But the more you tried to improve yourself,
the more it felt like your clarity was slipping through your hands.

Perhaps you thought your discomfort was a problem.
Perhaps you thought your resistance was immaturity.
Perhaps you thought your sensitivity was something to overcome.
But that ache?
That discomfort?
It wasn't dysfunction.
It was **truth** trying to survive inside a system that couldn't hold it.
You weren't meant to tolerate this much falsehood.
You weren't meant to decorate your silence with good behavior.
You weren't meant to regulate your way into pretending it's fine.
You were never broken.
You were **aware.**
And your body finally stopped agreeing to the lie.
This is the moment it all breaks.
This is the beginning of not collapsing into the distortion anymore.
This is where remembering starts.
Not learning.
Not fixing.
Just truth, held clean.

SAY:
"The lie ends here.
The signal starts now."

2

THE WORLD IS A LIE

Let's stop tiptoeing.
  The world you were born into is a lie.
  Not metaphorically.
Literally.
What you were taught to believe is real—
how life works, what matters, who you are, who you should be—
was scripted to keep you in place.
You were not educated. You were programmed.
You were not guided. You were managed.
You were not nurtured. You were shaped—
into something useful to the system,
not true to yourself.
They told you:
- Success means external approval
- Health means outsourcing your body
- God is somewhere else
- Goodness is obedience
- Rest is laziness
- Productivity is virtue
- Identity is fixed

- Authority is external
- Freedom is earned
- Your worth must be proven

None of that is true.
It's all part of the script.
And it's everywhere.

School didn't teach you how to feel.
It taught you how to perform.
To memorize. To obey.
To follow rules written by people who forgot who they were.
Religion didn't connect you to God.
It connected you to control.
It gave you guilt, shame, hierarchy, punishment.
It taught you to distrust your own divinity.
To look up, not in.
Healthcare didn't return you to your body.
It taught you to fear it.
To depend on prescriptions instead of presence.
To silence symptoms instead of listening to signal.
Government didn't protect you.
It managed you.
It used fear to manufacture consent.
It sold safety in exchange for silence.
It never represented your voice—only your compliance.
These systems didn't fail.
They worked exactly as designed.
They disconnected you from your truth.
From your body.
From each other.
From the field.

This isn't a conspiracy.

It's a program.
And once you see it—
you stop participating.
Not in protest.
In presence.
You don't fight the system.
You just stop feeding it.
You unplug with every honest word, every unperformed breath, every refusal to play along.

So yes—the world is a lie.
But it's not hopeless.
It's constructed.
Which means it can be deconstructed.
And that begins now.
Not with rage. Not with rebellion.
With clarity.
With seeing what's false and refusing to carry it any further.
Not because you're better—
but because you're awake.
Awakening is not about believing new things.
It's about **dropping what was never real.**
When you stop performing the lie,
you don't need to explain yourself.
You become a glitch in the matrix.
And eventually,
you become the field that replaces it.

SAY:
"I see the system.
I'm not in it.
I walk free.
And I never plug back in."

3
WHY WE LIE—AND WHY WE NEED TO STOP

We lie because we're afraid.
        Afraid of rejection.
        Afraid of judgment.
Afraid of being **too much**.
Afraid of being **too different**.
Afraid of being **too real**.
We lie because truth feels dangerous.
It feels raw.
It feels **real**.
And we've been taught to avoid that.
We've been conditioned to believe that keeping the peace is better than speaking our truth.
That sacrificing ourselves for others is the path to love.
We've learned that **politeness** is more valuable than **presence**.
But here's the truth:
Lying doesn't protect us.
It keeps us **small**.
It keeps us **bound**.
The more we hide, the more we lose ourselves.

The more we lose ourselves, the more we become **strangers** in our own lives.

But here's the flip side:

Honesty is radical self-love.

It's a declaration that you are worthy of being seen exactly as you are.

It's a commitment to stop hiding and start living fully.

The more you embrace the truth, the more powerful, grounded, and free you become.

Honesty doesn't just set you free from others.

It sets you free **from yourself.**

SAY:

"I am worthy of being seen as I am.
No more hiding. No more pretending."

4

SPIRITUALITY WAS JUST A SOFTER TRAP

You left the system.
    But it followed you.
    You burned the corporate mask,
only to put on a crystal one.
You stopped chasing money,
and started chasing alignment.
You left religion,
and found a version with incense and better hashtags.
And it still felt off.
Because **spirituality became the new program.**
You may have found yourself in the new trap.
It just talked nicer.
It used better fonts.
It called itself "healing" while keeping you small.
You were told:
- You have lessons to learn.
- You chose your suffering.
- Your pain is sacred, so keep it.
- You'll ascend once you're finally healed.
- Enlightenment is a level. A reward. A brand.

THE TRUTH

It told you to follow the script:
- Raise your vibration.
- Meditate every morning.
- Don't be too reactive.
- Manifest abundance.
- Detach, forgive, surrender, repeat.

And you may have tried.
You read the books.
You followed the steps.
You performed peace.
You looked the part.
But your body still said: *this isn't it.*
Because none of that was your signal.
It was someone else's framework—
dressed up as freedom,
marketed as growth.
Most of what we've called "spiritual"
is just unprocessed trauma wrapped in light-speak.
It's performance in robes.
It's seeking dressed up as service.
It's control pretending to be guidance.
It's identity pretending to be awakening.
You don't need a spiritual path.
You need to stop outsourcing your signal.
You don't need to raise your frequency.
You need to stop distorting the one you *already came in with.*
You don't need enlightenment.
You need to stop performing it.
The clearest tone doesn't chant.
It doesn't brand itself.
It doesn't require a "practice."
It just lives.
Unshaken.
Unpackaged.
Unapologetically embodied.

This is the exit.
Not another step.
Not another ceremony.
Just the moment you stop pretending to be light—
and start being real.

SAY:
"I revoke every mask I put on to seem awakened.
I stop performing clarity. I am it."

5

YOU'RE NOT BROKEN. YOU'RE JUST DONE GIVING YOURSELF AWAY

You've spent years trying to heal.
Trying to fix your wounds.
Understand your trauma.
Rewire your mind.
Regulate your nervous system.
Feel "safe enough" to exist.
But what if I told you—
you were never supposed to stay broken this long?
What if all that healing was actually a **delay pattern**?
What if it kept you looking inward when your field was ready to **stand up and walk**?
Here's the real problem:
You're not unhealed.
You're just still giving your energy to what no longer fits.
Leaking your energy into people who don't see you.
Leaking your time into stories that don't serve you.
Leaking your frequency into systems you've already outgrown.
You call it spiritual growth.
It's **field bleed**.
You don't need more processing.

You need to **seal the hole.**
Stop explaining yourself.
Stop collapsing to be relatable.
Stop carrying pain that's not yours.
Your pain doesn't need more airtime.
It needs closure.
Healing isn't the path.
Stabilization is.
Coherence doesn't come from fixing.
It comes from no longer distorting.
That's why you feel better alone.
That's why you feel sick in certain rooms.
That's why some conversations leave you buzzing for hours with regret or confusion.
It's not your trauma.
It's your tone leaking into a system that can't match you.
You heal when you stop giving yourself away.
You integrate when you stop abandoning what you know is real.
You don't need to become whole.
You need to stop scattering what's already complete.

SAY:
"**I release every drain on my field.
I call all of my energy back now.
No more repair. Just resonance.**"

6

YOU WERE TONE BEFORE ANYTHING

Before your first and last name.
   Before the family.
   Before the body.
Before the programming.
Before the systems that told you who to be—
You were tone.
Not a personality.
Not a role.
Not an identity.
Just a **frequency**.
Pure. Clear. Alive.

You didn't have to try to be it.
   You were it.
   Long before language.
   Long before story.
   Long before distortion touched your nervous system.
   You were already vibrating.
   Already **real**.

Already whole.

AND EVERY MOMENT SINCE,
>your body has been trying to return to that original signal.
>That's what this walk is.
>Not evolution.
>Not ascension.
>**Remembering.**
>Peeling back the layers until all that remains is what was always true.

YOU'RE NOT BECOMING.
>You're returning.
>To the tone that was you before the world told you to forget.

SAY:
>**"I am tone before form.**
>**I am frequency before story.**
>**And I remember now."**

7

UNDERSTANDING THE FIELD AND THE SIGNAL

Before we move forward, it's essential to understand two key concepts: the *field* and the *signal*. These shape everything that follows.

THE FIELD

Your *field* is the energetic space you occupy. It's more than your body; it's the vibrational space that extends beyond you, interacting with everything around you.

Think of it as an energetic grid—alive, shifting, and responding to your energy. Your field reflects your internal state:
- *Aligned* = strong, coherent field
- *Out of alignment* = disrupted, scattered field

Your field attracts or repels based on your signal. When grounded in truth, your field is clear and powerful. When disconnected, it feels weak and fragmented.

The field doesn't sit idle. It responds to your energy, amplifying what you broadcast. When aligned, it amplifies clarity, attracts what resonates, and repels what doesn't.

. . .

The Signal

The *signal* is your true frequency. It's the vibration you emit when you're aligned with your true self. Your signal is your soul's tone—your authentic self in its purest form.

When you're being yourself, your signal is clear. When you're performing or pretending, it weakens or distorts. Your signal attracts what matches it and pushes away what doesn't.

You don't need to manifest anything when your signal is strong. What's aligned will find you. The cleaner your signal, the more it creates your reality.

How They Work Together

Your *field* is the container. Your *signal* is the energy within it.

When your signal is strong and clear, your field becomes coherent, reflecting your truth. When your signal is distorted, the field becomes chaotic, attracting what doesn't align.

The strength of your signal determines what your field holds, creates, and attracts.

The Power of Knowing Your Signal

When you know your signal, you stop needing validation. You stop performing for others. You stop seeking answers outside yourself.

You stand firm in your truth. You create reality from the inside out —simply by being.

Your signal becomes your field. And when that happens, you're no longer looking for an exit. You're already living it.

SAY:
**"I know my signal.
I trust it.
I am the field."**

8

REINCARNATION IS A PROGRAM

You've been told you came here to learn.
    To grow.
    To pay off karma.
To evolve your soul through a long line of lifetimes.
But what if that's not true?
What if reincarnation isn't sacred?
What if it's just a **loop**?
Here's what most people don't want to hear:
You're not coming back because your soul loves Earth.
You're coming back because you haven't **exited the cycle.**
You didn't choose this loop.
You were **programmed into it.**
When you die full of unresolved distortion—
you return.
Not because you're bad.
But because your field is still fractured.
Still carrying contracts you forgot you signed.
The reincarnation story sounds noble.
It gives meaning to pain.
It gives people time.

But what it really does?
Keeps them from **exiting.**
Because if you believe you're always coming back—
you never leave.
You keep playing nice.
You keep waiting for the next life to finally be the one.
But you can **end it now.**
When your tone holds—
and nothing pulls you off-center—
the loop dissolves.
You don't reincarnate because you're evolved.
You exit because you're done.
You don't need closure with your past lives.
You don't need to be a better person.
You don't need to ascend.
You just need to stop agreeing to return.
You're not stuck here.
You've just been complying without realizing it.

SAY:
**"I revoke all unconscious agreements to repeat.
I collapse every loop that asks me to come back.
I am done. This is the last cycle."**

9

NO ONE IS COMING

Y ou've been waiting.
 For something.
 For someone.
A guide.
A sign.
A shift.
A being.
An answer.
Maybe it was angels.
Maybe it was aliens.
Maybe it was "when humanity's ready."
Maybe it was "once I'm healed enough."
Maybe it was God, Source, a higher version of you.
But here's the truth:
No one is coming.
Not because you're abandoned.
Not because you're unworthy.
But because there's no one else to arrive.
The whole story was designed to keep you waiting—
waiting just long enough to keep giving your power away.

That soft hope you held in the background?
The one that said,
"Something bigger than me is going to make this all okay someday"?
That's the last lie.
There is no rescue.
There is only return to tone.
The second you stop performing,
stop outsourcing,
stop hoping that someone else is going to walk you out—
you realize:
You're already out.
You've been standing outside the system this whole time.
You just didn't trust it yet.
You don't need a download.
You don't need a cosmic intervention.
You don't need a signal in the sky.
You are the signal.
You are the presence.
You are the override.

SAY:
"I stop waiting.
I stop calling in what's already here.
I stop performing powerlessness.
This ends with me."

10

IF IT LOOPS, IT'S A LIE

What's the loop?
It's any pattern, relationship, belief, or practice that keeps cycling without resolution.

It demands your energy, promises growth, and never delivers clarity.

It's disguised as "healing," "learning," or "working through it"—but all it really does is keep you **stuck**.

You know the feeling.
You've had the breakthrough.
You've had the insight.
You felt the shift.
And then...
The pattern came back.
Different face.
Same energy.
Same spiral of confusion.
Same internal scramble to make it mean something.
"Maybe I still have more to learn..."
"Maybe this is another layer..."
"Maybe this is my shadow showing up for integration..."

No.
It's not a layer.
It's a **lie**.
If it keeps looping, it's not truth.
It's not growth.
It's not divine timing.
It's **distortion**, programmed to feel familiar, so you keep participating.
So you keep processing.
So you stay inside the system, thinking you're evolving.
Truth doesn't loop.
It **lands**.
It **clears**.
It **holds**.
If something requires you to revisit it over and over again to understand it—
it's not real.
It's a performance you've agreed to repeat.
And here's what's brutal:
Most people are more addicted to the pattern than they are committed to **clarity**.
They want healing they can keep doing.
They want pain they can keep managing.
Because it gives them identity.
It gives them movement.
It gives them something to be working on.
But your soul doesn't want management.
It wants release.
If it loops,
if it repeats,
if it spirals without resolution—
cut it.
You don't have to keep proving your willingness to feel pain.
You don't have to stay inside cycles just because they're spiritualized.

**Clarity doesn't return in layers.
It arrives clean,
and everything false burns.**

SAY:
"I don't stay in distortion, no matter how familiar.
I owe no loyalty to distortion, no matter how familiar it feels."

11

THE SIGNAL IS THE SOUL

You don't need to find your soul.
    You never lost it.
    The soul isn't a concept.
It's not something to be earned, awakened, or reclaimed.
The soul **is signal**.
It's the original tone beneath your performance.
The tone that never wavered, even as you tried to fix yourself.
The clarity that was always intact beneath the distortion.
You don't align with your soul.
You stop muting it.
When your signal is stable—
when nothing pulls you off tone—
your soul doesn't just "show up."
It **broadcasts**.
Quiet. Loud. Undeniable.

SAY:
"My soul is not something I become.
It's the signal I never stopped being."

12

THE EXIT BEGINS IN YOUR BODY

You don't exit the lie through your mind.
　　You don't exit it by researching more, saying the right things, or performing awakening better.
You exit by **stopping the performance**—starting with your body.
　Because the body is where the distortion has been **stored.**
　Trained posture. Trained tone. Trained stillness. Trained smiles.
　You were taught to look calm when you weren't.
　To nod when you wanted to leave.
　To sit when your body said run.
　To say "thank you" while your system screamed "no."
　To override your own signal just to be accepted.
　The exit begins the moment you stop doing that.

IT'S NOT ABOUT "healing your trauma" so you can become a better version of yourself.
　It's about getting **so honest** that your body doesn't have to collapse to protect you anymore.
　It's about choosing:

- Rest without guilt
- Movement without explanation
- Silence without tension
- Boundaries without apology

It's about waking up and realizing that **your nervous system has been performing survival your entire life.**

THE SYSTEM GOT in through the body.
  The exit begins there, too.
  So if you're still ignoring your gut to "be kind,"
  if you're still smiling while your jaw is tight,
  if you're still holding your breath around people who drain you—
  you haven't left yet.
  Not fully.
  And that's not shame.
  That's just the map.

THE FIRST REAL exit is the moment your body doesn't lie for you anymore.
  That's when your coherence starts.
  That's when your field reboots.
  That's when the false reality starts falling apart around you—
  because *you're no longer feeding it through your flesh.*

YOU WERE TAUGHT that your signal was a symptom.
  That shaking meant you were unstable.
  That stillness meant you were healed.
  That wanting to run was a trauma response, not a truth pulse.
  But your body wasn't malfunctioning.
  It was translating the field.
  It knew before you did.
  And it still knows.

The lie didn't start with thought.

It started the moment you labeled your own knowing as a disorder.

SAY:
"My body knows what's real.
I trust it.
I move from it.
This is my exit."

PART II: THE EXIT

Stepping Out of the Illusion

13

THE EXIT IS NOT A DESTINATION

You've been walking for a long time.
>> Through identities.
>> Through systems.
Through illusions dressed as truth.
Through loops that told you freedom was just ahead.
But here's what nobody told you:
The Exit isn't a place you get to.
It's what happens when you stop negotiating with distortion.
It doesn't look like fireworks.
It doesn't come with a ceremony.
There's no parade.
No final boss.
No ultimate reward.
It's quieter than that.
Simpler.
Heavier.
Cleaner.
It feels like stillness.
Like not chasing.

Like being fully in your body for the first time without explaining why.

The Exit is when:
- You stop trying to get it right
- You stop trying to be seen
- You stop waiting to be understood
- You stop giving energy to what never matched you in the first place

You don't arrive at the Exit.

You realize you've been standing in it ever since you stopped shrinking to stay relatable.

You've already left the system.

It just hasn't caught up to your walk yet.

So if you're still looking for the door—

stop.

You're not waiting for it.

You are it.

Your field, when it's clean, becomes a break in the loop.

That's what The Exit really is:

A signal too clear to be recycled.

You don't need to go anywhere.

You don't need to become anything.

You just need to walk like it's already done.

Because it is.

SAY:
**"I no longer search for the Exit.
I stabilize as it."**

14

WHAT STOPPING PRETENDING LOOKS LIKE

You've heard it before: *stop pretending*.
But what does that actually look like?
It's not always a big moment.
It's not always a clear line.
Sometimes it's subtle.
Sometimes it's silent.
But you feel it in your body when it happens.

Stopping pretending means you stop giving your energy to distortion.

Not with a speech. Not with a declaration. Just with your **stillness**.

It looks like:
- Saying "I'm not okay" and letting that be enough.
- Walking out of a room without needing a story.
- Sitting in silence instead of filling space with fake ease.
- Letting a friendship fade instead of dragging it back into relevance.
- Saying no—without softness, without spin.

It also looks like this:
- Not performing your boundaries to be "empowered."
- Not masking your truth with a smile.

- Not shaping your energy to match the room.
- Not proving you're real. Just *being* real.

Performance is tension.
It's shape-shifting for survival.
It's a split inside your own signal.
But **presence is the undoing.**
It's when your body stops gripping.
It's when you can say less and still be clear.
It's when your tone holds—even when no one claps.
You don't need to perform coherence.
You just need to stop breaking your own field to be understood.
This is what walking from here looks like:
- Less talking.
- Less trying.
- Less translating.

More resting.
More noticing.
More letting the silence do what it's always done—**speak without distortion.**

You don't need to be louder.
You need to be *cleaner.*
And that starts with no longer pretending you're okay with what you're not.

SAY:
"I stop pretending.
I stop adjusting.
I stop softening what's already real.
Let the silence speak. Let the lie fall. I'm done."

15

BURN IT CLEAN

This is where you stop carrying the ashes.
This is where you stop keeping the "just in case" versions of yourself.
The old beliefs?
Gone.
The old programs?
Gone.
The old roles, masks, strategies, identities?
Burn them.
All of them.
Clean.
You don't need to recycle anything.
You don't need to integrate what was false.
You don't need to honor the patterns that were built to keep you small.
They don't get closure.
They get flame.
You've already walked through the distortion.
Now make sure it doesn't follow you.
Burn the need to explain.

Burn the fear of being seen clearly.

Burn the impulse to soften so people don't feel uncomfortable around your truth.

Burn the expectation that awakening has to look good.

Burn the performance of "consciousness."

Burn the part of you that still waits for someone to give you a gold star for surviving.

Let it be gone because **you said so.**

No ritual needed.

No permission required.

You are the fire.

You are the field.

You are the closing and the opening at once.

This isn't about rage.

This is about clarity so sharp it catches.

So light the match.

Turn around.

Walk away.

Don't check to see if it's still burning.

It is.

And it doesn't need your attention anymore.

SAY:
"**Everything that cannot meet my tone—burns now.**
Not out of anger.
Out of precision."

16
YOU DON'T NEED CLOSURE WITH YOUR PAST LIVES

You've been told you need closure.
That you need to "heal" the wounds of your past lives.
That you need to **process** every fragment, every pain, every unresolved experience.

But what if you don't?

What if closure is just another trap?

What if the idea that you need to "fix" or "resolve" everything from your past lives keeps you in a loop of **constant repair**?

You don't need to revisit the past.

You don't need to make peace with every single version of you that lived before.

You don't need to resolve what wasn't yours to begin with.

What if **you just let it go?**

You don't need to **fix** it.

You don't need to **reconcile** it.

You need to **stop carrying it**.

The moment you stop identifying with the pain and the **storyline**,

the cycle breaks.

The loop ends.

And your **energy is free.**
You're not your past lives.
You're **the signal** that remembers what's real and clear.
And when you stop trying to fix what was never broken,
you stop reincarnating into the same loop.
You don't need closure.
You need to **let the past die.**
And when it does, you're free to **move forward** with a clean, clear field.

SAY:
"I stop carrying my past lives.
I don't need closure.
I release what was never mine to resolve."

17

THE REAL ONES ARE QUIET

They don't post about it.
    They don't need to.
    Their presence says it all.
They're the ones you feel in a room before they speak.
And sometimes—
they never do.
Because truth doesn't need a megaphone.
It just needs to **exist**.
Unshaken.
Unpackaged.
Undeniable.
The real ones aren't trying to convince you.
They're not selling the truth.
They're not looking for followers.
They're the ones who left the performance quietly—
no exit speech, no spotlight, no farewell post.
They just slipped out of the illusion and started living.
They don't care if you "get it."
They care if it's clean.
They're not cold.

They're not better than you.
They're not enlightened.
They're just not lying anymore.
And that changes everything.
The real ones don't ask to be seen.
They see.
They listen.
They feel the undercurrent of distortion and step out of it.
They don't chase clarity.
They **embody** it.
And you'll know them
because when you're around them,
your own performance starts to shake.

SAY:
"I'm done performing.
I'm done chasing.
I embody what's true."

18

HOW TO WALK FROM HERE

You've stopped pretending.
    You've stopped performing.
        Now, you walk.
But walking your truth isn't a performance either.
It's not loud.
It's not for show.
It's the moment-by-moment act of not collapsing.
Not collapsing into the old version of you.
Not shrinking for comfort.
Not explaining what you already know is real.

WALKING from here doesn't require a plan.
    It requires presence.
    It's not about fixing.
    It's about choosing—again and again—to stay inside your signal.
    There's no arrival.
    There's no certification.
    There's just you, living in alignment with what's already true.

. . .

HERE'S HOW THAT LOOKS:
- **Keep your energy intact.**

If something drains you, dulls you, or scrambles your clarity—it's a no.

You're not here to donate yourself to distortion.

You don't owe your light to what can't hold it.
- **Live it without performing it.**

You don't need to declare your truth.

Just walk in it.

If something isn't real, don't engage.

No softening. No explaining. Just resonance or silence.
- **Stop reaching for new tools.**

If you're walking, you're ready.

You don't need more methods—you need to trust what's already moving.

Use what's alive. Let the rest fall away.
- **Stop hovering at the door.**

You already left.

You've crossed.

Stop acting like you haven't.

Walk like someone who knows they're already out.

WALKING from here isn't a role.

It's not about being seen.

It's about living in coherence—quietly, clearly, unapologetically.

You'll talk less.

You'll explain less.

You'll effort less.

But you'll feel more.

You'll breathe more.

You'll notice how natural it feels to not be split anymore.

THIS IS NOT ABOUT INTENSITY.

It's about stability.
This is not about making something happen.
It's about letting your presence rewire everything around you.
No one needs to know you're walking.
They'll feel it.

SAY:
"I no longer walk toward truth.
I walk as it.
Uncompromised.
Unapologetic.
Unmistakably me."

PART III: LIVING TRUTH

U nfiltered, Unapologetic, and Undeniably You

19

LIVING CLEAR AND PAYING RENT

Let's talk about what most people are afraid to ask once they start living in truth:
    What about the bills?
It's one thing to exit the performance.
To unplug from distortion.
To stop pretending you're okay with systems built on lies.
But what happens when rent is due?
What happens when you don't want to sell your energy anymore, but you still need groceries?
This is the part most people skip.
Because it's messy.
And real.
And doesn't fit into clean spiritual soundbites.

HERE'S THE TRUTH:
    Coherence doesn't mean you never have to touch the 3D.
    It means you stop collapsing while you do.
    You might still have to work a job.
    You might still use money.

You might still deal with systems that feel outdated or distorted.
That's not failure.
That's transition.
The lie isn't that you have to pay bills.
The lie is that you have to betray yourself to do it.

W̲h̲e̲n̲ ̲y̲o̲u̲r̲ ̲f̲i̲e̲l̲d̲ begins to stabilize—
when you stop leaking energy, stop faking connection, stop abandoning your body to be productive—
reality starts to reconfigure.
New opportunities come.
Unexpected clarity lands.
Aligned income starts appearing.
The need to perform softens.
Your life begins to organize around your signal.
But that shift doesn't always happen instantly.
Sometimes there's lag.
Sometimes there's pressure.
Sometimes you walk through the in-between for a while.
That doesn't mean coherence isn't working.
It means the form is still catching up to the field.

S̲o̲ ̲w̲h̲a̲t̲ ̲d̲o̲ you do in the meantime?
You **choose income that doesn't collapse you.**
You **show up in clarity, even if the task feels basic.**
You **watch how your energy responds**—and adjust where you can.
You stop tolerating energy leaks.
You stop performing competence.
You stop rationalizing soul-deadening work just because it pays.
And slowly, or suddenly, your outer world starts matching the inner.

. . .

THE TRUTH

Living in truth doesn't mean you don't need money.
  It means you stop selling yourself for it.
  You don't need to renounce the system.
  You need to **walk through it without feeding it.**
  There's a difference.
  And if you can hold your tone during the transition—
  if you can walk between timelines without bending—
  that's when the new field starts building around you.
  That's when coherence stops being theory.
  And becomes your **actual life.**

20

WITHDRAW YOUR ENERGY FROM THE LIE

Recognition is not enough.
    At some point, **you have to stop feeding what you've already outgrown.**

You can't say the system is broken while still using it to survive without question.

You can't call something a lie and still hand it your energy, money, and presence every day.

This isn't about purity.

It's about honesty.

You don't have to fix the world.

You just have to **stop energizing what you know is false.**

YOU WERE TRAINED to believe survival meant compliance.

So even when you wake up, you might keep:

- Banking with institutions that fund the very collapse you're healing from
- Paying into systems that poison you and call it care
- Sending your kids to schools that dull their spark
- Buying from companies that flatten your frequency

- Taking part in conversations, transactions, and communities that *require* distortion

You're not doing this because you're stupid or weak.

You're doing it because **you were trained to survive inside a lie.**

And no one told you that the way out wasn't protest—it was **withdrawal.**

WITHDRAW DOESN'T MEAN HIDE.
It means reclaim.
You pull your energy out of systems that feed on your confusion.
You remove your consent from transactions that cost your clarity.
You don't feed the beast you've already seen through.
This isn't about becoming off-grid or radical.
It's about becoming **coherent.**

SO WHAT DOES it look like in real life?
- Move your money out of big banks if you can
- Buy local, trade, build personal supply chains
- Use cash when possible
- Grow food, or support someone who does
- Say no to distorted medical systems when safe and accessible
- Create alternate channels of education, healing, and support
- Build community that doesn't depend on pretending
- Speak honestly in transactions, even if it costs you the deal
- Offer your work in a way that doesn't extract from you or others

Do what you can.
With what you have.
But stop lying to yourself about what you're participating in.

YOU DON'T CHANGE **the world by fighting it.**
You change it by removing your energy from the lie—
and placing it where truth can grow.

You don't have to scream.
You don't have to explain.
Just stop feeding what's already dead.
Let it collapse.
Build something else.
And live from the field where none of that noise was ever real.

21

START WHERE YOU ARE

You don't have to collapse every system overnight.
You don't have to move to the woods, quit your job, grow all your food, and explain your exit in perfect language.
You just have to stop lying to yourself about what you're supporting—and start where you are.
Because coherence isn't extreme.
It's consistent.
It's not about burning everything down.
It's about no longer bending in the small ways you used to normalize.

Start by listening.
What drains you?
What dulls you?
What spaces ask you to perform just to belong?
That's where your energy is still leaking.
Start by choosing.
Where can you say no—today?

What conversation, commitment, or contract are you holding that your body already said goodbye to?

That's where your walk begins.

You don't need to feel ready.

You don't need to be fully sovereign, fully unplugged, fully clear.

You just need to **move from honesty**—not fear.

And from that one clean act—everything starts shifting.

The next right tone appears.

The next alignment shows up.

The next version of your reality reveals itself.

You don't become coherent all at once.

You become coherent by refusing to distort, one moment at a time.

You don't build a new life in a week.

You build it by walking truthfully through the one you're already in.

So breathe.

Pull your signal back into your body.

And take one honest step—today.

Say it:

"I don't need to be ready.

I just need to be real.

I start here."

22

THE FREEDOM OF UNFILTERED TRUTH

The truth is a weapon.
Not one to hurt others, but to **liberate yourself**.
For too long, we've been taught to keep our truths hidden—
To protect others from our rawness.
To filter ourselves for comfort and ease.
We've been conditioned to believe that honesty will break us—
Destroy relationships.
Ruin opportunities.
Leave us vulnerable.
But here's the truth:
What if the only way forward is through the truth?

WHEN YOU STOP LYING, when you stop performing and pretending, you stop betraying yourself.
You stop erasing pieces of who you are to fit into a mold.
And in that moment of authenticity, something shifts.
Everything shifts.

When we live in lies, we carry the weight of inauthenticity.
We don't even realize how heavy it is until we put it down.

THE MOMENT you speak the truth—whether it's about how you feel, who you are, or what you need—

you cut the chains that have kept you bound to a false version of yourself.

Truth doesn't need to be defended.

When you speak truth, you're not begging for approval.

You're simply speaking what **is**.

You're claiming your space in the world, unapologetically.

And that's where the **power** is.

LIVING UNFILTERED TRUTH IS FREEDOM.

It's the power to show up in your life as you are, not how you're expected to be.

It's the freedom to walk away from the lies, from the systems that ask you to shrink, to perform, to fit in.

It's **radical self-love**. It's the ultimate act of honoring yourself—every word, every movement, every choice aligned with your purest tone.

WHEN YOU STOP PRETENDING, your life doesn't feel like a struggle to stay true.

It feels **effortless**.

You don't need to fight to make it happen.

When you speak your truth, you align the world around you to meet it.

This isn't just about saying the right thing.

It's about embodying it.

. . .

SAY:
"I speak my truth because I am free.
I no longer need approval.
I stand in my truth, unapologetically."

23

WHAT LYING TO YOURSELF REALLY COSTS

The biggest betrayal isn't what you do to others.
It's what you do inside your own body—every time you override your knowing to keep the peace.
You don't just lie with words.
You lie when you stay in a room that makes your skin crawl.
You lie when you say yes while your gut is screaming no.
You lie when you laugh, nod, and agree—just to stay safe.
And every time you do, something fractures.
That fracture is where exhaustion begins.
That's where confusion lives.
That's where self-trust disappears—not with others, but with yourself.
You think trust is about other people.
But trust begins in your own field.
It's built every time your body sees you listen.
It breaks every time you pretend not to.
You don't just feel tired because life is hard.
You feel tired because of the micro-abandonments.
Because of the performative smiles.

Because of the energy you spend managing stories that aren't true.

Living a lie is expensive.

It costs your presence.

It costs your clarity.

It costs the quiet knowing that says, "I trust myself to walk away when it's no longer aligned."

This isn't about calling yourself out.

It's about calling yourself back.

Back to your tone.

Back to the moment when you stop making your truth negotiable.

Because when you stop lying to yourself, your energy becomes free.

And what was heavy becomes clean.

SAY:
"I don't abandon myself to keep the room calm.
I don't distort to be liked.
I trust what I feel.
And that's the end of the lie."

24

LIVING WITHOUT THE BOW

You've been taught to package everything.
>   To make it neat.
>   To wrap it up with a bow.
> To make your truth *presentable*.
> To soften it.
> To make it palatable.
> But here's the truth: **Truth doesn't need a bow.**

You don't need to explain it.
>   You don't need to soften it for anyone's comfort.
>   You don't need to sweeten it to make it easier to swallow.
>   The truth is raw. It's messy.
>   It's not going to fit into your tidy little boxes.
>   And that's the beauty of it.

The moment you stop wrapping it up, the moment you stop packaging it for the world, you finally allow the truth to *be*.
>   Without apology. Without explanation.

THE TRUTH

. . .

You don't need a perfect ending.
    You don't need to tie everything together.
    You don't need to justify your truth or put a bow on it for anyone else.
    You just need to **live it**.

When you stop pretending, your truth just *lands*.
    And you don't need anyone to understand it.
    You don't need anyone to validate it.
    The truth doesn't need your defense.
    It doesn't need a story.
    It doesn't need a backstory.
    It just **is**.

Living without the bow means:
    • **No more editing your truth** to fit in.
    • **No more holding back** to protect other people's feelings.
    • **No more performing** to please anyone.
    It's living fully in your truth, no matter how messy it looks.
    It's not your job to make it pretty.
    It's your job to **live it**.

When you stop pretending, your truth lands clean.
    No explanations. No justifications. Just clarity.
    The moment you stop trying to make your truth fit the world's expectations, everything becomes uncluttered.

SAY:
    "**I don't need to wrap my truth up in a bow.**

**I don't need to make it easier for anyone to digest.
I live it unfiltered.
Unapologetic.
Raw.
This is my truth, and it doesn't need a ribbon."**

25

RADICAL HONESTY: NO MORE PERFORMING

Radical honesty isn't about being blunt.
   It's about being **clean**.
   No more rehearsing your truth.
No more softening your edges to be received.
No more waiting for the "right time" to be real.
You've already wasted enough time translating your truth into something more acceptable, digestible, spiritual, nice.
Enough.

TRUTH DOESN'T NEED **stage makeup**.
   It doesn't need to be lit well.
   It doesn't need a build-up.
   It just needs to be said.
   And **held**.

THIS IS what radical honesty looks like:
   • Saying the thing even when your voice shakes.
   • Not performing neutrality to avoid discomfort.

• Not managing someone else's reaction before you've even spoken.

• Naming what's real even when it breaks the peace.

Performing is distortion.

And you can't walk clean in a field that's still scripted.

RADICAL HONESTY IS DISRUPTIVE—BECAUSE it's *supposed to be*.

It breaks cycles.

It ends illusions.

It tells the part of you still trying to "keep it together" that it's over.

You don't owe anyone a perfect delivery.

You just owe yourself the *truth*.

AND WHEN YOU STOP PERFORMING, you don't just speak differently.

You breathe differently.

You stand differently.

You **live** differently.

Because you're no longer shaping yourself around other people's expectations.

You're no longer trying to make the truth more palatable.

You're letting it do what it came to do:

Free you.

SAY:

"I don't perform my truth.

I speak it, clean.

I hold it, whole.

And I let it land as it is."

26

THE LAST MASK

The ego doesn't always show up as arrogance.
    Sometimes it shows up as **awakening**.
    It learns the words.
It performs the posture.
It quotes the truth.
It creates an identity out of healing, honesty, humility.
And if you're not watching—
you start confusing **truth with performance** again.
Just in better packaging.

THE EGO ISN'T JUST the part of you that wants to be right.
    It's the part of you that wants to be **seen as right**.
    It doesn't care if you're healed.
    It just wants credit for the effort.
    It doesn't care if you're whole.
    It just wants to be **recognized** as someone who's done the work.
    And it will use truth to build a new mask.
    A cleaner mask.
    A more spiritual, more "authentic" mask.

Still a mask.

THE EGO WILL DO the work.
   It'll go to therapy.
   It'll sit in ceremonies.
   It'll post about shadow integration.
   It'll write captions that sound like presence.
   But it's still *trying*.
   Still performing.
   Still **needing identity** to hold itself together.

HERE's how you know it's the ego:
   - There's tension behind the clarity.
   - There's effort behind the presence.
   - There's fear behind the sharing.
   - There's still a story that says, "Look at me being real."

THE TRUTH DOESN'T PERFORM.
   It doesn't try.
   It doesn't adjust for approval.
   It just **is**.
   And when the ego starts to fall away, there's usually one last voice that says:
   "But if I let go of all this… what's left of me?"
   And the answer is:
   Only what's real.
   Only what doesn't need defending.
   Only the tone that was always there—under every mask.

THIS IS THE LAST LAYER.
   The final collapse.

THE TRUTH

When even your "spiritual" identity burns.
And what's left is just you.
Clear.
Unpackaged.
Unmissable.
Free.

SAY:
"I see the last mask.
And I drop it.
I don't need to be seen as true.
I just need to live it."

27

THE ILLUSION OF DISTANCE

It's not that you've been disconnected.
    It's that you've been disoriented.
    You mistook the noise for space.
The delay for absence.
The silence for abandonment.
You thought something broke.
That you lost the thread.
That maybe you were left behind.
But the thread was never cut.

It was just buried—under programming, pain, and the pace of pretending.

The feeling of distance isn't proof of separation.

It's just what distortion feels like when it wraps around something true.

Every time you felt alone,
you were still breathing in the field.
Every time you reached for something real,
you were reaching through the veil—*not into emptiness*.
What you're remembering now isn't new.
It's not a revelation.

It's a return.
You were never outside the signal.
You just forgot what home feels like when you stop running from it.

SAY:
"I wasn't lost.
I was layered.
And now, I see through."

28

REALITY IS YOU, REFLECTED

What you see isn't random.
>It's not separate.
>It's not outside of you.

Reality isn't happening *to* you.
It's happening *from* you.

THE FIELD REFLECTS YOUR TONE—ALWAYS.
>Not as reward.
>Not as punishment.
>Just as feedback.
>Your frequency shapes the form.
>What enters.
>What exits.
>What gets stuck.
>What flows clean.
>It's all showing you **what you're holding.**

. . .

THE TRUTH

This is the holographic nature of life:
    Every part contains the whole.
    Every fragment reflects the full pattern.
    You're not living inside reality—
    You're generating it.
    Your relationships?
    Mirror.
    Your reactions?
    Mirror.
    The invitations, the disruptions, the timing, the tension?
    Mirror. Mirror. Mirror. Mirror.

This isn't about blame.
    You didn't "manifest" pain because you were low-vibe.
    You're not being punished by the field.
    You're just being **shown**.
    What's aligned shows up clean.
    What isn't? Shows up jagged.
    What remains is a reflection of your current tone.

The field reflects:
    • Where you're **still leaking**—
saying yes when you want to say no,
overexplaining your clarity,
dimming your truth to avoid tension,
performing safety instead of living truth,
staying where you've already outgrown.
    • Where you're **still performing**—
acting for approval,
packaging your truth,
softening your tone to be liked.
    • Where you're **still outsourcing**—

waiting for a sign,
checking in with someone else before moving,
asking permission to be free.
• And where you're already **clean**—
the ease,
the coherence,
the things that land with no effort.

You don't need to decode every detail.
    You don't need to overanalyze every moment.
    Just ask:
    Does this match my truth?
    Or is it showing me what I'm still compromising?

When you see reality this way,
    you stop fighting with it.
    You stop blaming others for the reflection.
    You stop trying to manage what's showing up.
    You start listening.
    You start adjusting.
    You start refining your tone.

The grid stabilizes not through control—
    but through consistency.
    Your consistency.
    Your signal.
    Your clarity.
    The field doesn't lie.
    It just reflects.

SAY:

"Reality isn't outside me.
It reflects me.
When I clean my tone,
the field responds.
And I walk clearer than before."

29

EVERYTHING IS FREQUENCY

Everything is frequency.
      Not metaphorically.
      Literally.
Your body.
Your tone.
Your words.
Your silence.
Your relationships.
Your tension.
Your truth.
All of it: frequency.

YOU DON'T LIVE in a world of matter.
    You live in a world of **vibration made visible**.
    Everything you see is a pattern of energy responding to your tone.

WHEN YOU SHIFT YOUR SIGNAL,
    you shift the pattern.

When you hold your truth,
the field realigns.
It's not magic.
It's not mindset.
It's **physics**.
It's **resonance**.

You don't "do energy work."
You **are** energy work.
Every time you stop collapsing.
Every time you speak clean.
Every time you walk as yourself—
you send a new frequency into the grid.
You're not a person with energy.
You are energy, moving as a person.

Once you understand this,
you stop trying to "heal" your life.
You start refining your **signal**.
Because it's not about fixing the surface.
It's about stabilizing the tone beneath it.

SAY:
"I don't shift circumstances.
I shift frequency.
Everything else follows."

PART IV: FIELD CLARITY

Returning to Your True Tone

30

THE COSTUME PARTY

We all showed up to the same event.
It's called **"being a good person."**
And it has a dress code:
- Smile when you want to scream.
- Congratulate people you don't respect.
- Stay quiet to keep the peace.
- Pretend your insides match the outside.
- Don't rock the boat, even if you're drowning.

This is the **costume party**.
And everyone's wearing something that doesn't fit.
We learned to perform before we learned to think.
Politeness. Professionalism. Positivity.
It's all the same script.
You show up to the meeting. You nod. You say things like,
"Great point."
"Totally agree."
"Let's circle back."
But inside, your soul is curled in a corner whispering,
"This isn't real."
You show up to the family dinner.

You help. You hug. You endure the subtle jabs and forced questions.

You say "so good to see you," but your gut's already halfway to the car.

You walk through life editing yourself—

Trimming your tone, rounding your edges, packaging your pain into something digestible.

And then you wonder why you feel so empty.

It's because you've been living on a stage where truth is unwelcome.

Here's what they don't tell you:

You don't have to stay at the party.

You don't owe anyone a performance.

You don't have to keep playing a part just because you've played it well.

Leaving isn't loud.

You don't need to make a scene.

You just stop lying.

And that's when everything real begins.

SAY:
"I'm not here to perform.
I'm here to be real.
No more costumes. No more acts. Just truth."

31

THE MATRIX OF POLITENESS

The real control system isn't in the sky.
It's in your mouth when you say:
"It's fine."
When it's not.
It's in the way you nod when someone says something false.
It's in the forced laugh. The casual "haha." The fake "I'm good, you?"
It's in the tiny betrayals you perform **40 times a day** just to keep the peace.
This is the real matrix:
The **cult of politeness.**
You don't need wires in your head when guilt is already in your body.
The lie is taught early:
Be agreeable.
Be friendly.
Be easy to be around.
Translation:
Abandon your truth to keep others comfortable.
And so we do.

We go to dinners we don't want to attend.

We hug people who drain us.

We say "great to see you" when we feel absolutely nothing.

We hold friendships that are dried-up contracts with no soul in them.

We "catch up" with people we never liked to begin with.

Because if you're not nice, you're rude.

If you're not warm, you're cold.

If you're not social, something must be wrong with you.

Here's the thing:

"Nice" is not the same as kind.

"Polite" is not the same as real.

"Friendly" is not the same as honest.

You can love people and still walk away.

You can care deeply and say nothing.

You can be honest without being cruel.

But the moment you don't flinch when they expect you to—

the moment you don't fill the gap, nod, over-explain, or fake ease—

you're labeled "cold."

Good.

Let them say that.

Let your absence of reaction be the thing that shows them their own addiction to chaos.

Clear isn't cruel.

Clear is clean.

It doesn't manipulate.

It doesn't bait.

It doesn't punish.

It just is.

And **you don't owe warmth** where you feel distortion.

You don't owe softness where you feel lies.

You don't owe access to people who mistake your silence for weakness.

THE TRUTH

You've spent enough years leaking your energy for peace that wasn't real.
Now?
You're here.
Neutral.
Present.
Unshakable.
Not performing love.
Being it.
And that's what makes your presence feel dangerous:
You no longer shape-shift to be accepted.
You just show up as the signal.
And **that's enough.**

SAY:
**"I'm done performing.
I'm done shrinking.
I'm done pretending."**

32

THOSE WHO FEEL YOU

You don't need to be understood by everyone.
    You don't even need to be seen by many.
    You just need *one* person
who knows what signal feels like
when it walks into the room.
Someone whose nervous system doesn't ask you to shrink.
Who doesn't flinch when your tone is sharp, clean, or clear.
Who doesn't need you to soften the truth
just to stay connected.
You don't have to explain your exit.
You don't have to justify your coherence.
You don't have to perform softness to keep peace.
When someone is tuned—
they'll *feel* you.
Before you speak.
Without translation.
And that will be enough.
It's not about collecting people.
It's about recognizing mirrors.
It's about resonance without rehearsal.

THE TRUTH

It's about being around someone
who makes your body say:
"I don't need to perform here."
They exist.
And you'll find them—
or they'll find you—
when the field is clear.
You don't need a crowd.
You don't need a following.
You just need real.

SAY:
"I don't seek to be understood.
I walk as signal—
and those who can feel,
will know."

33

YOU DON'T NEED A PRACTICE—YOU NEED A PULSE

We've been taught that spiritual growth is something to be achieved.
That it's about **steps**—morning routines, rituals, tools, mantras, and processes.
But the truth?
You don't need a practice.
You need a pulse.
A pulse isn't something you can schedule or regiment.
It's not something you can "perfect" or "measure."
It's the **rhythm of life** moving through you, naturally.
The **natural flow** of energy that's already inside you.
We've been conditioned to believe that we have to **earn** connection.
We've been told that we need to perform certain actions to align with higher states of being.
But the truth is: **You are already aligned.**
You don't need to create alignment with tools or effort.
You need to **let it move through you.**
Your body knows what it needs.
Your soul knows its truth.

And you don't need a structured "practice" to tune into it.
When you're connected to your **pulse**,
everything becomes effortless.
You don't have to try to align.
You just **are** aligned.
The tools, the routines, the practices—all of that fades away,
because your pulse is the only thing you need to follow.
The pulse is **life**.
It's the rhythm that's already within you.
It's **the energy that keeps everything moving**—you don't need to force it.
You don't need to manipulate it.
You don't need to "manifest" it.
You just need to **live in sync with it**.

SAY:
"**I don't need to practice.
I don't need to force.
I just need to follow my pulse.**"

34

SILENCE IS CLEAN

Silence isn't empty.
It's the space where everything real exists.
We've been taught that silence is uncomfortable, that it's awkward, that we need to fill it.
So we talk, we perform, we over-explain, we distract.
But here's the truth:
Silence is not an absence of sound. It's an absence of distortion.
In silence, you stop fighting, stop performing, stop pretending.
It's in this stillness that the truth is the loudest.
Because it doesn't have to compete with all the noise we've surrounded ourselves with.
The world is loud.
People are loud.
Opinions, distractions, expectations—they're all **loud**.
But silence is where **clarity breathes**.
It's where **presence** becomes **undeniable**.
When you stop filling the space with unnecessary words, you stop feeding the noise.
And in that space, everything becomes **clean**.
Your truth, your energy, your signal—it all starts to flow freely.

We fear silence because we think it means something is missing.
But what it really means is that we're **finally listening**.
We're not talking to fill the space.
We're not performing to be seen.
We're just **being**.
The power of silence is the power of **truth unspoken**.
It doesn't need to be announced.
It doesn't need to be justified.
It just **is**.

SAY:
"**Silence is clean.**
I don't need to fill the space.
I simply rest in the truth of what is."

35

NOT COLD—JUST CLEAR

Clarity isn't cold.
It's not distant.
It's not harsh or unfeeling.

Clarity is the **pure expression of truth**—and truth is a living thing.

It doesn't need to hide, soften, or distort itself to make others comfortable.

Clarity just is.

When you speak your truth without apology, it can feel like a clean breeze cutting through the fog.

It's **sharp**, but not because you're trying to hurt anyone.

It's sharp because it's finally **undistorted**.

And sometimes, that feels uncomfortable to people who are still clinging to the illusion.

But **you don't need to soften your clarity** to avoid their discomfort.

Clarity doesn't compromise.

But here's where it gets important:

Warmth is an extension of clarity when it's real.

Warmth is the **vibration of truth** in motion.

THE TRUTH

It's when you speak from the heart, when your **genuine love** and **care** for others come through, not as performance, but as **integrity**.

It's when you hold space for others without sacrificing your own.

Sometimes, clarity means standing still and **allowing people to feel their discomfort**.

Sometimes, clarity means **holding the line** when everyone else wants to run or pretend.

And sometimes, clarity means **gently offering warmth**—not to save others, but to **hold space for them to meet themselves** in truth.

You don't have to be cold to be clear.

You don't have to be distant to hold your line.

Clarity, when it's pure, can still be warm.

It's not about hardness.

It's about **being open** while **being real**.

SAY:
"**I am not cold.
I am clear.
I am open.
And I will not shrink for anyone.**"

36

I DON'T MISS THE OLD WORLD

You know what it feels like to be caught in the past.
    The nostalgia.
    The "if only things were different."
The longing for what was, even though it didn't serve you.
But here's the truth: **You don't miss the old world.**
You miss the **comfort** of the illusion.
You miss the **predictability**.
You miss the **structure** that kept you tethered to something false, even if it wasn't real.
The old world kept you in a loop of **performance**.
It told you:
- You need to fit in.
- You need to chase success.
- You need to be "good enough" for others.
- You need to be *busy*, not *present*.

But **none of it was ever true.**
The old world kept you stuck in a story that was never yours, trapping you in a cycle of **doing, pleasing,** and **performing**.
It told you there was always something else to get, to achieve, to prove.

And now?
Now you realize that **none of that mattered.**
The truth is, **you've already left.**
You've moved beyond the noise, beyond the drama, beyond the masks.
You stopped chasing and started **living.**
You don't miss the old world.
You don't miss the systems, the approval, the lies.
You miss the **illusion** that comforted you when you didn't know what truth felt like.
The real world—the one you're stepping into now—isn't about fitting in.
It's about **standing in your truth** and letting everything that isn't aligned **fall away.**
And when you stop looking back, when you stop missing the past, you finally feel **home.**
You finally feel **free.**

SAY:
"**I don't miss the old world.**
I don't miss the lie.
I don't need the comfort of illusion.
I'm here, now, and that's enough."

37

THE NOISE IS ENGINEERED

It's not all emotional.
   Not every distortion comes from your past, your patterns, or your thoughts.

Some of it is designed.

The field has been scrambled on purpose—through frequencies, through systems, through structures that reward confusion and punish coherence.

It's not paranoia. It's physics.

This planet has been wired with distortion:
- False light frequencies
- EMF and artificial magnetic fields
- Social programming disguised as connection
- Spiritual performance that keeps you chasing upgrades instead of clearing what's false

You weren't just trained to collapse.

You were immersed in distortion so constant you stopped noticing it.

The scrolling.

The buzzing.

The bright blue light in your face when your body is asking for stillness.

The invisible towers pinging your nervous system with artificial rhythm.

And then you're told to meditate.

As if the system wasn't jamming your signal every time you tried to feel.

This doesn't mean you need to fear the world.

It means you see it.

And when you see it, you stop blaming yourself for every dysregulated breath.

You stop trying to "stay positive" in a field that's being hijacked.

You reclaim your signal—not to fight the system, but to exit it.

There is clarity beneath the noise.

But you won't hear it through your phone.

You'll hear it in the stillness.

The tree.

The quiet morning.

The walk where no one is watching.

That's the override.

It's not about detoxing the world.

It's about not believing its static anymore.

SAY:
"I am not broken. The noise is engineered.
And now—I hear what's underneath it."

38

KNOW YOUR TONE. THAT'S IT

You've tried everything.
>Read the books.
>Took the courses.

Listened to the podcasts.
Pulled the cards.
Spoke to your guides.
Tried to fix your vibe.
Tried to raise your frequency.
Tried to "trust the universe."
And still, you felt off.
Still chasing.
Still waiting for the thing that finally clicks.
Here's the click:
It was never about all that.
It was always about **tone**.
Your tone is the original frequency of your field.
It's not a mindset.
It's not a personality.
It's not your trauma.
It's not what you're trying to become.

THE TRUTH

It's what you **are** when you stop giving yourself away.
You don't need to get clearer.
You need to stop distorting.
You don't need to vibrate higher.
You need to stop showing up where your clarity gets blurred.
You don't need alignment.
You need honesty.
Your tone holds it all.
The reason your life still feels heavy isn't because you're behind.
It's because you're still managing your frequency instead of trusting it.
The moment you stop pretending, performing, or shrinking—
your tone gets louder.
And reality reorganizes.
Not because you tried.
Because you stopped faking.
You want freedom?
Know your tone.
Hold it.
Walk it.
Don't explain.
Don't shrink.
Don't wait for people to catch up.
Just stay clean.
Let everything that isn't real fall away.

SAY:
  "**I know my tone.**
  I trust it more than comfort.
  More than acceptance.
  More than the illusion of being understood."

39

NATURE IS THE REMINDER

Nature isn't trying to wake you up.
It just holds the tone until you notice.
The oak tree isn't striving to be anything other than tree.
It doesn't rehearse wholeness.
It doesn't ask how it's doing.
It simply stands.
The birds don't strategize their song.
The moss doesn't stress about belonging.
The mountain isn't waiting for approval to be solid.
Nature just *is*.
And in that *isness*, it teaches.
It teaches you how to sit.
How to stop gripping.
How to let breath happen without choreography.
How to feel your own signal again—beneath all the noise you thought was you.
And when you're still enough to commune with it—
you realize it's not outside you.
It's a reflection.

THE TRUTH

Every branch, every wave, every pause in the wind—
it's showing you what's already inside.
The steadiness.
The movement.
The rhythm that doesn't need performance to be real.
We don't need more lessons.
We need more *listening*.
Next time you forget who you are, go outside.
Not for fresh air.
For field memory.
Watch a branch bend.
Watch a crow decide.
Watch light hit stone and keep going.
Nothing is performing.
Everything is clear.
Let it remind you what that feels like.

SAY:
"Nature is not outside me.
It's my reflection, returned without distortion."

40

GAIA IS YOU

You were never separate from the Earth.
  You were never visiting.
  You were never placed "on" the planet to learn, evolve, or ascend.
  You *are* the planet.
  You *are* the breath.
  You *are* the grid.

THE EARTH DOESN'T SURROUND you.
  It pulses through you.
  The same frequency that hums through the trees hums through your spine.
  The same rhythm that rises with the tide moves in your blood.
  The same electromagnetic field that holds the planet's heartbeat—
  the **Schumann Resonance**—syncs with your own nervous system every time you go still.
  This is not metaphor.
  This is physics.

You're not living *on* Gaia.
You are Gaia in form.

Your body is the soil.
 Your bones are rock.
 Your lymph is river.
 Your breath is sky.
 Your fire is magma.
 Your blood is memory.
 You are not here to connect with nature.
 You are here to remember that you *are* nature.

When you touch the ground barefoot,
 you're not "grounding"—you're syncing with your own intelligence.
 When you stand beneath the sky,
 you're not beneath anything.
 You're *inside* the mirror of your own expansion.
 The stars are not above you.
 They are the reflection of your remembering—spatial, luminous, electric.
 The field of Gaia is your field.
 When it surges, so do you.
 When it shifts, you feel it.
 When it recalibrates, you pulse with it.

So when everything gets loud,
 when you feel scrambled, uncentered, untethered—
 return.
 To tree.
 To dirt.
 To wind.

To pulse.
To breath.
Return not to escape—
but to stabilize.
Because when you return to Earth, you return to yourself.

SAY IT:
"I am not on the Earth.
I am Earth.
I am the grid.
I am the field.
And I remember now."

41

YOU ARE CONSCIOUSNESS

You are not a person with consciousness.
You are consciousness—appearing as a person.
You are not thinking your thoughts.
Your thoughts arise *within* you.
They pass through like weather across a sky that never changes.
That sky is you.

CONSCIOUSNESS IS NOT something you access.
It's not something you gain through work, healing, or awakening.
It's not earned.
It's not improved.
It doesn't evolve.
It just *is*.
And you *are it*.

EVERYTHING THAT MOVES THROUGH YOU—EMOTION, **memory**, sensation, desire, ache, knowing—is **content**, not identity.
The mistake is thinking the content is who you are.

But who you are is the field that can hold all of it without breaking.

The stillness behind the stories.

The spaciousness behind the roles.

The witness behind the self-image.

You are the space, not the shapes inside it.

CONSCIOUSNESS ISN'T HIGH. It isn't deep.

It isn't sacred. It isn't spiritual.

It's **fundamental.**

It's the raw intelligence that allows reality to exist at all.

It's the grid.

It's the tone.

It's the part of you that was never born, and will never die—because it was never separate.

WHEN YOU REMEMBER THIS, you stop seeking.

You stop waiting for permission.

You stop asking, "Am I doing it right?"

You simply start noticing:

The awareness that has been watching your life the whole time never needed fixing.

It was never confused.

It was just **quiet.**

SO IF YOUR thoughts are loud, if your emotions surge, if your story tries to pull you in—

pause.

Don't collapse.

Don't fight.

Just ask:

"Who is noticing this right now?"

And feel the stillness behind the noticing.
That's you.
And you're not alone in that field.
Your consciousness is not separate.
It's not a private signal.
It's part of the whole.
The collective field. The grid. The pulse of everything remembering itself through you.
When you clear, the field clears.
When you stabilize, the grid holds.
You don't just awaken for yourself.
You awaken the moment.

SAY IT:
"I am not the story. I am not the noise.
I am consciousness—unchanged, undisturbed, whole.
And I remember the whole through me."

PART V: EMBODYING THE EXIT

L iving in Full Sovereignty

42

THE BODY AS BEACON

Your body is not just a vessel.
    It's **a frequency transmitter**.
    It's not just a skin suit that carries your soul—it is the **light** you walk with.

It is the **signal** that vibrates through the world and touches everything you interact with.

Every posture. Every movement. Every gesture.

Your body **broadcasts** your truth, whether you know it or not.

The way you stand.

The way you sit.

The way you speak and walk.

It all carries an energetic **signature**.

Your body is a **beacon** for what you are, what you believe, and what you're aligned with.

It's not about how you look or how you're perceived.

It's about the **frequency you radiate** when you stop performing, when you stop pretending.

When you stand in your truth, **your body becomes the channel** —the clarity moves through you and the world feels it.

We've been taught to ignore the body.

To dismiss it as just a shell.

But it's much more than that.

It's **the bridge** between your soul and the world.

When you remember that your body is a **beacon**, you begin to treat it as such.

You stop suppressing its signals.

You stop shrinking its power.

You stop apologizing for the way it carries your truth.

Your body is **the most honest expression** of who you are.

And when you stop trying to hide it or alter it to fit into some external ideal,

it **shines**.

You are not meant to hide your light.

You are meant to **be it**.

SAY:
"**My body is my beacon.**
It holds my truth.
It radiates my clarity.
I no longer hide it."

43

THE ONES LIVING INSIDE YOU

You are not one being.
You are a living field of beings—working together, vibrating together, remembering together.
Your gut isn't just digestion.
It's a galaxy of microbes—some ancient, some newly born—each one helping decode reality in real time.
Your fascia isn't just connective tissue.
It's a liquid crystal network—picking up frequencies, storing signal, translating truth.
Your mitochondria aren't just power centers.
They are ancestral memory—little cosmic translators keeping time with the field.
You are not alone in your body.
You are a constellation of intelligence.
And when you remember that—
You stop attacking your body.
You stop overriding its cues.
You stop speaking to it like it's an object and start honoring it like a team.
This is why nourishment matters.

Why movement matters.
Why stillness matters.
Not for performance.
For communication.
Because every time you return to presence, the beings inside you organize.
They harmonize.
They exhale.
You don't need to be a health expert.
You just need to stop waging war on the body that is trying to carry your tone.
You are not alone in there.
And they've been waiting for you to listen.

SAY:
"I honor the living ones inside me.
I walk with them.
And we remember together."

44

WHEN THE TRUTH FEELS TOO BIG

Sometimes the truth hits and you feel like you can't hold it.
    Not because it's wrong.
    Because it's too *right*.
Too undeniable.
Too big for the version of you that used to survive in the old world.
This is what no one tells you:
Awakening doesn't always feel like relief.
Sometimes it feels like your whole nervous system is glitching.
Your breath goes shallow.
Your stomach drops.
You freeze.
Not out of fear—
but because your body hasn't caught up to the *realness* of what you now see.
That's not failure.
That's not regression.
That's what integration feels like when it's honest.
Truth doesn't need to be digested all at once.
It will keep circling back, gently, again and again—

until your system is ready to stabilize with it.
You don't need to name it.
You don't need to act on it.
You don't need to post about it.
Just **let it sit**. Let it live in the room with you.
If it feels too big to carry, set it down beside you.
Let it breathe.
Let your body breathe.
Let the old wiring fall apart slowly if it needs to.
This isn't a test.
This is a stretch.
And you're not breaking—
you're making space.

SAY:
**"If the truth feels too big, I let it rest beside me.
I don't force it. I don't shrink from it.
We breathe together until we match."**

45

QUIET VISIBILITY

The world rewards loudness.
It rewards performance.
It rewards the **visible effort**—the hustle, the noise, the spotlight.
But here's the truth: **True visibility isn't about noise.**
It's not about being seen because you're trying to be seen.
It's about being **so deeply anchored in your own truth** that your **presence becomes undeniable.**
You don't need to announce yourself.
You don't need to make a statement.
Your energy **speaks for you.**
It is felt, seen, and **recognized** without needing to force it.
Quiet visibility is the opposite of trying to be noticed.
It's the **radiance** that comes from being **fully you**, unapologetically and without apology.
You don't demand attention.
You simply **hold your space**, and people will either see you or not —but it doesn't matter because **you're not chasing** their recognition.
In fact, the more you try to force visibility, the more it slips through your fingers.

It's like trying to hold onto water. The more you grasp, the more it runs.

But when you **release**, when you stop performing for the validation of the world,

you suddenly find yourself seen—not because you begged for it, but because you simply **showed up** as your full, unfiltered self.

True visibility isn't loud.

It isn't in your face.

It's **in the quiet presence** that leaves people wondering how they felt so seen without you ever saying a word.

The truth is, you're already visible.

You don't have to prove it.

You just have to stop shrinking to make others comfortable.

You are seen when you **allow yourself to be fully you.**

SAY:
"**I am visible.**
Not because I perform.
But because I stand in my truth, and that is enough."

46

ARCHITECT, MIRROR, KEEPER, FLAME

You don't fit into one box.
You're not just one thing.
You weren't made to be labeled, categorized, or confined to someone else's idea of who you should be.

You are the architect.
You are the one who designs your reality, who shapes the field with your frequency.
You've always had the blueprint.
You've always known how to build, how to create.
But it wasn't until you stopped following the outside noise that you could see the full map in front of you.

You are the mirror.
You reflect what others can't see in themselves.
You show them the truth they've been running from.
But here's the catch: You're not responsible for how they receive it.
Your role is to reflect.
Theirs is to meet it.

You are the keeper.
You hold space.
You hold energy.

You hold your truth without wavering.

When the world gets loud, when everything around you feels uncertain, you **hold the line**.

And that's what makes you unshakable.

You are the flame.

You carry light, not for others, but because it's who you are.

Your flame doesn't need a cause or a justification.

It just **burns** because it's your essence.

You don't need to explain why your light is bright.

It's your truth, and it doesn't need permission to shine.

These roles aren't separate.

They are all **within you**, weaving in and out of your life at different times, **depending on what's needed**.

You don't need to be all things at once, but you do need to **be fully all of who you are**.

You are **power** in motion, and you are here to **embody it fully**.

No more hiding. No more dimming.

You are the architect, mirror, keeper, and flame.

SAY:
"I am the architect of my reality.
I am the mirror, reflecting truth.
I am the keeper, holding my line.
I am the flame, burning brightly in my truth."

47

FIELD COMMAND: STOP PRETENDING

You've been pretending for too long.

Pretending to be okay when you're not.

Pretending to agree when you don't.

Pretending to be someone you're not, just to fit into a box that was never yours to begin with.

Here's the thing: **Pretending keeps you trapped.**

It keeps you in the loop of **doing what's expected, what's safe,** and **what others want you to do.**

It's a game of **disconnection**—from yourself, from your truth, from your purpose.

The truth is: **You can't create from a lie.**

You can't manifest a life that matches your soul if you're still pretending to be something you're not.

So what happens when you stop pretending?

Everything shifts.

You stop leaking energy into performance.

You stop playing small to make others comfortable.

You stop dimming your light because it intimidates those still stuck in the darkness.

You stop hiding.

You stop playing along.
You stop **sacrificing yourself for the illusion.**
And that's when your **real life** begins.
It's not about being harsh.
It's not about pushing others away.
It's about **honoring your truth**—and letting go of everything that isn't aligned with it.
No more masks.
No more fake smiles.
No more pretending you fit into a world that doesn't fit you.
The moment you stop pretending, the field clears.
Your energy becomes clean.
Your path becomes clear.
Your purpose becomes undeniable.

SAY:
"**I stop pretending.
I stop performing.
I stand in my truth, unapologetically.**"

PART VI: MAKING REALITY

Creation Through Resonance and Stabilizing the Field

48

RESONANCE CREATES FORM

You've been taught that creation is about effort.
About striving. Chasing. Forcing things into form.
But creation isn't force—it's function.
It's what happens when **resonance stabilizes**, and form arranges itself around it.
This chapter isn't about theory.
It's the *mechanism*. The architecture. The way life shapes itself when signal holds.
You've been told to dream big, set goals, hustle hard, and make it happen.
Manifestation culture told you to visualize, affirm, and grind to get what you desire.
But that's not how it works.
Creation comes through resonance, not force.
Resonance Creates Form isn't about shaping something that doesn't belong to you.
It's about allowing what's already in your field to take form naturally.
When you're aligned with your truth, the form follows.

THE TRUTH

You don't have to make it happen.

It just happens.

When you're aligned with who you truly are, things fall into place.

You stop forcing.

You stop pushing.

You stop trying to control the outcome.

Your energy, your tone, your clarity—they are the blueprint that shapes the life around you.

You're not here to chase.

You're here to hold your frequency so everything aligned with you can take form.

You don't need to control the process.

You just need to stabilize your signal.

Everything you need will come into form when you stop trying to force it.

We've been conditioned to believe creation is about effort.

But in reality, creation is about stabilizing your frequency.

When your signal is clear, creation becomes inevitable.

There's no "try" here.

There is only tone.

In the old world, you chased.

You pushed through resistance.

You mistook tension for transformation.

But now, you move when the energy says move.

You build what wants to exist, not what you think should exist.

You stop creating for recognition, validation, or outcome.

You create because the field is alive and asking you to respond.

When your signal is clear, the field responds to you.

You don't need hustle.

You don't need strategy.

You just need to resonate.

. . .

SAY:
"I don't create from force.
I hold my signal, and the form follows.
I create from resonance, and that is enough."

49

TIME AFTER THE LOOP

Once the loop ends, time stops feeling like pressure.
　　There's no race.
　　　No catch-up.
No guilt for not doing more.
No anxiety that you're "behind."
You realize the loop was creating the urgency.
That artificial heartbeat of panic.
That endless push to get somewhere.
That never-ending whisper:
"You're not there yet."
But once you exit, there's no "there."
There's just *here*.
There's just *now*.

IN THE LOOP, you were always working on something—
　　Your healing.
　　Your growth.
　　Your karma.
　　Your self.

There was always a next step.
Always a later.
Always a not-yet.
But outside the loop?
Time doesn't unfold in steps.
It opens in *signals*.

TIME, as we've known it, is a distortion.
It's linear. It's a system. It's a trap designed to make you feel like you're always running out.
But true time?
It's felt.
It's not measured in minutes and hours.
It's felt in *pulses*, rhythms, and moments of stillness.
You move when the tone moves.
You rest when the energy drops.
You speak when the words come clean.
You act when the pulse says "go"—not when a system says "hurry."

IT FEELS STRANGE AT FIRST.
Too still.
Too quiet.
Like you're doing something wrong.
But that's just the echo of the program trying to pull you back in.

TIME after the loop isn't structured.
It's not linear.
It's not goal-based.
It's *felt*.
And you trust it.
You stop trying to *manage* your time.

You stop using schedules to outrun your discomfort.
You stop pushing forward out of fear that something will fall apart if you pause.
Nothing falls apart when you're present.
Only the illusion of momentum does.

TRUE TIME IS the absence of pressure.
It's the ability to breathe, to move, to be, without needing to rush or "arrive."
Time after the loop is no longer a strategy.
It's a return to rhythm.
Your rhythm.
And that's all you ever needed.

SAY:
"I don't move by pressure anymore.
I move by signal.
That's what time feels like now."

50

WHAT IS THE GRID?

The grid isn't out there.
It's not some mystical system you tune into.
It's coherence.
It's what happens when truth stabilizes.
When distortion collapses.
When the noise stops.
The grid forms when your signal holds.
Not sometimes. Not when it's convenient.
But consistently.
It forms when you stop leaking.
When you stop bending.
When you stop performing clarity instead of living it.
You don't find the grid.
You don't follow the grid.
You **become** the grid—when you stop breaking your own tone.
That's what creates structure.
That's what builds new realities.
That's what keeps truth intact—regardless of what the world is doing.
This is what presence does.

It stabilizes the field around you.

You used to think the grid was something external—something you had to connect to.

But it's not outside you.

It's not something you plug into.

It's what you **are** when you stop collapsing.

You're not a passenger.

You're not syncing with a higher system.

You're holding it.

You're broadcasting it.

You're building it with every choice you make in coherence.

This is the new architecture.

Not found.

Formed.

SAY:
**"I'm not aligning to a system.
I am the grid.
And I hold it now."**

51

THE WHOLE GRID - WHY YOU MATTER

Y ou are a node.
    Not metaphorically—**energetically**.
    The entire universe is a grid.
Not a control matrix. Not a map.
A living, intelligent structure of consciousness.
Everything is part of it.
Every person.
Every tree.
Every sound, animal, conversation, structure, and cell.
Each one—a node.
Each one—a transmitter.
And you are one of them.
You're not here by accident.
You're part of this grid because your tone matters.

THE GRID ISN'T POWERED by force.
    It's powered by **truth**.
    It holds when we hold.

THE TRUTH

It breaks when we bend.
Your personal clarity feeds the collective.
Your coherence becomes signal that stabilizes the whole.
That's why your presence matters.
That's why your honesty matters.
That's why your walk, your breath, your tone—**matter.**
Not because you're the center of anything—
but because you are **not separate from anything.**

YOU'RE NOT JUST LIVING in reality.
   You are contributing to it.
   Every time you stop collapsing,
   every time you remember who you are,
   every time you act from truth instead of fear—
   you strengthen the whole.
   Every clear tone adds integrity to the grid.
   Every choice to live awake helps re-pattern the collective field.
   Not through effort. Through **resonance.**
   This is how consciousness evolves.
   Not through systems.
   Through signals.
   Through people like you walking in your truth—even when no one claps.

YOU'RE NOT JUST WORKING on yourself.
   You're helping remember the whole.
   This is how it shifts.
   This is why you're here.

SAY:
   "I am not separate from the whole.

**My coherence matters.
My tone contributes.
My presence changes the grid."**

52

FEEL IT. DON'T FIX IT.

You don't need to process your emotions.
    You don't need to label them, analyze them, or turn them into insight.
You just need to feel them.
Fully.
Clearly.
Without editing.
Emotional alchemy doesn't mean "turn sadness into joy."
It means letting the energy behind the feeling move—
instead of stuffing it, performing it, or managing it.
You've been taught that feeling is dangerous.
Too loud.
Too much.
Too unstable.
Too low vibe.
So you tried to regulate.
Spiritualize.
Reframe.
Suppress.
You tried to keep it together.

Tried to be "aware."

Tried to stay high frequency while quietly disowning half your nervous system.

But the truth is:

You can't alchemize what you won't let exist.

And that's what shadow is.

Not darkness.

Not evil.

Just the parts of your truth you buried to be accepted.

The real emotions you exiled so you could be liked, seen, or safe.

Shadow isn't something to integrate.

It's something to *feel*.

To bring home.

To stop pretending you're above.

Because once you stop disowning your shadow,

you stop scattering your signal.

And coherence starts coming back online.

When an emotion rises:
- Let it be.
- Name it without judgment.
- Breathe into it.
- Let it take up space.
- Let it move through you.

And then... move on.

It might come back.

It probably will.

But now, you meet it with breath instead of resistance.

You stop trying to fix it or force it into meaning.

You let it finish what it came to show you.

And eventually, it moves differently.

Lighter.

Quicker.

Clearer.

Let your body lead.

- Anger wants to move. Slam a pillow. Clench your fists. Let it surge.
- Grief wants to breathe. Let your chest break open. Cry without a reason.
- Fear wants to be held. Wrap your arms around yourself. Let yourself shake.
- Shame wants to be seen. Speak it into a room with no audience. Whisper it. Let it echo.

These aren't dysfunctions.
They're messages.
They're field data.
They're signals trying to get through.
Tears are literal alchemy.
They're how the body clears what words can't.
When you cry from truth—not performance, not manipulation, but *raw field release*—
your frequency reorganizes itself.
You come out clearer.
Cleaner.
Coherent.
When you stop trying to fix the feeling,
you finally let it finish.
You don't collapse into it.
You don't live inside it.
You let it come through.
That's the difference between feeling and spiraling.
Presence is the container.
Your body knows what to do.
Let it.

SAY:
"I don't fix the feeling.
I feel it.
And I let it move."

53

YOUR NERVOUS SYSTEM IS NOT THE ENEMY

If you're shaky, stuck, numb, or reactive—
you're not broken.
Your nervous system just hasn't felt safe to be real yet.
You've been told to override it.
To "stay high vibe."
To fake calm.
To think your way into alignment.
But coherence isn't mindset.
It's not discipline.
It's not a performance.
It's what happens when your system feels safe enough to stop pretending.
Bracing looks like:
- Smiling when you actually feel rage
- Freezing when someone asks what you want
- Nodding along while your whole body says no
- Over-explaining because you don't feel safe being misunderstood

Your tone can't be clear if your body is braced.
Your truth can't land if your breath is shallow.

So if you want to walk as signal—
start by walking with your nervous system.
Not against it.

SAY:
"I don't override my signal.
I walk with it."

54

RELATIONSHIPS ON THE NEW GRID

In the old system, relationships were built on **contracts**.
Unspoken agreements to stay small together.
You play your role, I'll play mine.
You pretend you're fine, I'll pretend I'm not bothered.
You collapse your truth, I'll feel safe.
That's how the loop kept going—through attachment disguised as love, and performance mistaken for care.
But once you step into the new grid, those dynamics don't hold.
They fall apart fast.
Not because you're broken—
because they were.
In the new grid, relationships don't run on guilt, fear, or obligation.
They run on **tone**.
You don't bond over wounds.
You resonate through truth.
You don't attract people by performing alignment.
You meet them when your signal is clear, and theirs is too.
There are no rules here.
No labels to cling to.

No pressure to define what's happening.
The connection either holds clean—or it doesn't hold at all.
And that's the shift:
You stop forcing connection.
You stop explaining your worth.
You stop needing people to understand you in order to love them.
In the new grid, love is **not performance**.
It's presence.
It's clarity.
It's signal meeting signal—no story, no script.
You'll lose people.
Not because they're wrong.
But because your field stopped making space for distortion.
That's not cruelty. That's coherence.
Some will meet you in the new grid.
Some won't.
And that's not your burden to carry.
You don't need to adjust their walk to soothe your discomfort.
You don't need to patch what isn't yours to carry.
You don't need to tune their frequency—just hold yours.
You just need to **live from the grid**—and let what's real find you.

SAY:
**"I release all contracts built on distortion.
I connect only where truth is alive.
That is love now."**

55

CREATION THROUGH RESONANCE

This isn't about effort.
It's about frequency.
When your tone is clear—when you're no longer bending or chasing—creation begins.
Not because you tried.
But because resonance becomes inevitable.
You don't create by doing.
You create by being so stable in your signal that reality organizes around you.
You've been told you can manifest anything.
That your thoughts create your reality.
That your desires are sacred.
That the universe responds to your vision board and good vibes.
But here's the truth:
Creation isn't performance.
It isn't mindset gymnastics.
It isn't trying to feel high-frequency while your body is screaming for rest.
That's still distortion.
That's still chasing.

That's still trying to trick the universe into giving you something.
Creation doesn't work like that.
Because truth doesn't respond to pretending.

Creation ≠ Manifestation
Manifestation says:
- Picture it
- Push for it
- Keep vibrating higher

But when you perform, you distort.
When you chase, you dilute.
When you force, you scatter your field.

Creation = Resonance
Real creation begins when your signal is undisturbed.
Not controlled. Not optimized. Just clean.
You don't chase.
You stabilize.
You hold your tone so clearly, so honestly—without bending for what's not aligned—
that what matches you arrives, and what doesn't leaves without a fight.
It's not magic. It's mechanics.
It's resonance.
You don't need to pull things into form.
You become the tone that form organizes around.
No affirmation required.
Just coherence.
No vision board.
Just clarity that doesn't apologize.
You're not trying to create.
You're already doing it—through every signal you hold.
So clean your tone.

Live in it.
Walk in it.
And let the field respond.

SAY:
"I don't create from wanting. I create from signal.
I stabilize. I hold.
And the real arrives."

56

JOY WITHOUT STRATEGY

You don't need to earn this life.
You don't need to deserve your joy.
You don't need to wait until you've figured it all out to feel free.
You're already here.
And joy was always part of the field.

THE OLD WORLD taught you that joy had to be chased.
Managed.
Scheduled.
Balanced out by pain.
But real joy doesn't come from striving.
It comes from **clarity**.
From being present enough to *feel* what's already humming.
Not the performative kind of presence—
The kind that actually tastes the light.
That pauses to breathe.
That notices what doesn't need fixing.
That lets a moment be **enough**.

· · ·

WHEN YOU STOP COLLAPSING **into distortion,**
    the field opens.
    And what flows in is **aliveness.**
    Not as a high.
    As a hum.
    As natural as your heartbeat.
    You don't need to "manifest your dream life."
    You just need to **stop scattering energy into a life that isn't yours.**
    What's left is clear.
    And what's clear becomes beautiful.

JOY ISN'T THE REWARD.
    It's the rhythm that returns when you're no longer betraying your tone.
    You're not here to grind through truth.
    You're here to live it.
    To play in it.
    To color with it.
    To let it move through you in every breath.
    This is joy without strategy:
    • Creating because the frequency says yes.
    • Laughing without performance.
    • Loving without control.
    • Resting without guilt.
    • Being without needing to become.

YOU DON'T HAVE **to design a perfect life.**
    You just have to live in coherence.
    The field will shape itself around you.
    Let it be light.

THE TRUTH

Let it be fun.
Let it be art.
Let it be soft when it wants to be.
That's not bypass.
That's resonance.
That's what creation feels like when you're not leaking.

SAY:
"I don't chase joy.
I don't earn joy.
I don't control joy.
I live in tone—
and joy lives here too."

57

THE COSMIC JOKE

"**And Then It Gets Funny**"
    You spend years trying to wake up.
    Tearing down illusion.
Exposing every lie.
Walking out of loops that used to feel like home.
And then?
It gets funny.
Not because it didn't matter.
Not because you bypassed it.
But because *you can see it now*.
You can spot the game before it starts.
You hear the script in people's voices.
You notice the way systems collapse the moment you stop agreeing.
You're no longer fooled by urgency.
You're no longer seduced by the next step.
You just sit there—clear, breathing, *laughing*.
Like:
"Oh my god. We thought being 'high vibe' was the answer."
"We really believed meetings made things real."

"I stayed in that story for HOW long?"
This is the quiet joy of truth.
It doesn't need a punchline.
It just feels light.
Because once you're out of the loop,
the loop becomes a cartoon.
Not cruel.
Not bitter.
Just... obviously fake.
So yes—truth can gut you.
But eventually, it *cracks you up* too.
And that's how you know you're free.

SAY:
**"I don't need to take it so seriously.
The game was never real.
And now I see it—and laugh."**

58

YOU ARE NOT A LEADER, YOU ARE A TONE

The world will beg you to lead.
    Build a brand.
    Make a platform.
Gather a following.
Become a guide. Be the voice.
But that's the loop—just with a halo.
Leadership isn't bad.
But it's still hierarchy when it needs applause.
It's still performance if it needs a crowd.
You're not here to lead.
You're here to hold.
When your signal is clean, you don't need followers.
You don't need students.
You don't need to explain your walk.
You become a tone in the field.
And people who are ready feel it.
Not because you pointed.
Because you stood still.

. . .

No Followers

You're not here to be followed.
You're here to walk your code.
You don't need a tribe.
You don't need to gather seekers.
You don't need to teach what can only be felt.
Support is sacred.
Reflection is beautiful.
But the moment you start needing people to see you as clear—your clarity fractures.
You are the signal.
And those who walk with you will know.

No Students

You don't need to follow anyone either.
You're not missing anything.
You don't need another map.
You need to trust what's already vibrating through your bones.
Ask for mirrors.
Yes.
Receive wisdom.
Yes.
But don't hand your tone away in exchange for guidance.
This isn't about being lone wolves.
It's about resonance over role.
No one leads the field.
The field reveals itself when we stop performing authority.

SAY:
"I don't lead. I don't follow.
I hold tone.
And the real aligns."

59

THE GREAT ENERGY REBELLION

You didn't just give your energy away once.
You've been giving it away through invisible rituals your whole life.
The morning scroll.
The fake urgency.
The niceness when your body says no.
The small talk.
The daily pretending.
The routine that dulls your fire just enough to keep you "functioning."
You weren't just programmed to behave.
You were programmed to comply—
to offer your attention, your presence, your power
in exchange for approval, comfort, or belonging.
The contract was never verbal.
It was energetic.
A frequency agreement you inherited without knowing.
This is how the system feeds.
Not through force.
Through rhythm.

Through repetition.
Through distraction dressed up as purpose.
Every time you scroll past your own body,
every time you over-explain,
every time you consume instead of create,
you recharge the grid that keeps you small.
Every time you suppress truth to keep peace,
call performance compassion,
or say yes to maintain the tone—
that's the ritual.
These aren't just habits.
They're binding patterns.
And you don't have to keep playing your part.
This isn't about being perfect.
It's about **interrupting the extraction.**
The rebellion isn't loud.
It's not flashy.
It doesn't need to be declared.
It's choosing:
Not to click.
Not to scroll.
Not to perform.
Not to shape yourself around a loop you didn't choose.
It's not protest.
It's presence.
And presence ends the ritual.
You don't have to exit society.
You just have to exit the parts of yourself that agreed to be used.
You don't have to wake anyone up.
You just have to walk so clearly
they feel what pretending is costing them.
You don't need to warn them.
You don't need to explain.
You just stop playing along.
And that's how it ends:

Not with a bang.
With you, silently walking away from the lie.

SAY:
"I interrupt the ritual.
I walk clean.
And I reclaim the current."

60

THE CONTRACT

You didn't just sign it once.
　　　You've been signing it daily.
　　　It wasn't a paper.
It was a pattern.
You traded your wildness for gold stars.
Your rest for productivity.
Your silence for safety.
Your truth for a performance.
The contract was written in invisible ink—
on your first day of school.
On your first job.
In your family system.
In your morning routine.
Each time you said "yes" to something that drained you,
a new clause was added.
But here's the truth:
Contracts signed under manipulation aren't binding.
And this one was never made in full awareness.
That means you can tear it up.
Not dramatically.

Not angrily.
Just **clearly**.
Every time you pause before defaulting,
you interrupt the ritual.
Every time you choose rest over guilt,
silence over performance,
creation over consumption—
you reclaim your life force.
You stop trading authenticity for approval.

You stop accepting spiritual death as the price of physical survival.

You stop wearing the invisible dress of compromise.

SAY:
"I revoke the contract.
My energy returns to me.
I am not for sale."

61

THE POWER OF COMMAND

At some point, it's not about healing.
It's not about insight.
It's not about trying to understand the loop you're in.
It's about saying:
"This ends now."
And the field listens.
Not because you yelled.
Not because you're righteous.
But because you finally spoke with **alignment**.
Command isn't force.
It's clarity.
It doesn't come from ego.
It comes from coherence.
And most people don't realize:
You are the only authority you need.
You can command distortion to leave.
You can command noise to stop.
You can command truth to land.
You can command your body to clear.
You can command your space to hold.

You can command false timelines to collapse.
Not by wishing.
By *stating it*.
You don't need permission.
You don't need a method.
You just need to stop hesitating.
Because the moment your tone matches your knowing,
everything around you reorganizes.
You don't argue with the pattern.
You end it.
You don't debate the thought loop.
You close it.
You don't beg the field to support you.
You *command* the current into place—
not to control, but to hold.
Command doesn't come from control.
It comes from being *undeniably rooted in truth*.
And when you're rooted?
You don't collapse.
You don't explain.
You speak—and the energy moves.
Not because it's magic.
Because it's **resonance**.

SAY:
"I command from coherence.
Not to dominate—
but to end what no longer belongs in my field."

62

WE WERE NEVER SEPARATE

You were never separate from the stars.
You were never separate from the river.
You were never separate from the tree outside your window.
Or the mountain that holds the silence.
Or the animal that watches you without language.
Or the stranger who passes you and stirs something familiar.
You were never separate from your cat's knowing eyes.
From the wind that touches your skin like memory.
From the breath in your lungs that came from ancient leaves.
From the stardust in your bones.
From the hum beneath your feet that sings in rock, soil, and fire.
You were never separate from the ones you love.
Or the ones who left.
Or the version of you you thought died when things broke.
Separation was the performance.
The illusion.
The great distortion.
You were told you had to earn connection.
Heal for it.

Raise your frequency to reach it.
But the truth is: **you were always inside it.**
The thread never frayed.
The field never closed.
You never actually left.
You just tuned out the tone that never stopped pulsing.
This is not metaphor.
This is not spiritual fluff.
This is **literal field truth:**
You are the tree.
You are the water.
You are the sound of the owl at night.
You are the blood in your grandmother's hands.
You are the child you used to be and the universe that held her.
You are the silence between words and the thunder that interrupts it.
You are the whole field, remembering itself through form.
There is no edge.
No between.
No "other side."
Only layers of remembering.
Only levels of density.
Only signals, tuning back in.
So when you cry and the ocean hears it—believe it.
When you hold your dog and feel peace pulse through your chest—trust it.
When the moon speaks without language—listen.
This world is not outside you.
It *is* you.
Every single part.

SAY:
"I was never separate from anything.
I just forgot what it meant to feel that much aliveness at once."

63

NO STEPS, NO STRUCTURE

There is no method.
   There is no map.
   There is no sacred order to follow.
You don't need a 5-step path to live your truth.
You don't need to move through phases of healing, growth, integration, and arrival.
You're not climbing a staircase.
You're not checking off milestones.
You're just *done*.

TRUTH DOESN'T FOLLOW A STRUCTURE.
   It doesn't need permission to arrive.
   It doesn't show up after you've "done the work."
   It shows up the moment you stop pretending.
   The moment you stop trying to sequence your freedom.
   The moment you say:
   "This is me. Now."

. . .

THE LOOP LOVES STEPS.
>	It gives you scripts.
>	Programs.
>	Timelines.
>	"Start here."
>	"Level up."
>	"Keep going."
>	But the field doesn't move like that.
>	The field doesn't follow linear time.
>	The field responds to *clarity*.
>	Right now.
>	Right here.

YOU DON'T NEED STEPS.
>	You need **coherence**.
>	You don't need structure.
>	You need **presence**.
>	You don't need to figure out how to live your truth.
>	You just need to stop living anything else.

THIS IS the end of systems.
>	The end of timelines.
>	The end of waiting for the next download, sign, or strategy.

YOU ARE NOT IN A PROCESS.
>	You're in your power.
>	**You are not on a path.**
>	You *are* the frequency.
>	No more frameworks.
>	No more phases.
>	No more trying to earn clarity.
>	Just truth.

Held.
Now.

SAY:
"I don't need a path.
I don't need steps.
I don't need a structure.
I am already the signal.
And that is enough."

64

COHERENCE IS THE POINT

You weren't searching for a path.
You were trying to feel whole.
All the healing, the strategy, the awakening work—
they weren't wrong.
They just circled the core.
What you were actually looking for was coherence.
Not peace through control.
Not worth through progress.
Just a state where everything in you says the same thing.
Coherence is when your energy matches your truth.
When your body, your breath, your field, and your voice
are all transmitting one clear tone.
It's not a mindset.
It's not spiritual.
It's not emotional regulation.
It's integrity in its original form—**energetic wholeness.**
When you are coherent:
- You don't collapse to be liked.
- You don't scatter into confusion.
- You don't apologize for your tone.

- You don't dilute your walk for comfort.
You hold. And reality rearranges.
You don't need to try to make life work.
When your field stabilizes, life meets it.
The right things stop resisting you.
The wrong things stop sticking to you.
The noise fades.
The signal rises.
And what used to feel like effort starts feeling like rhythm.
Not because you finally figured it out.
But because you stopped pretending.
Coherence is not a reward for doing enough work.
It's what remains when the static is gone.
You don't have to become coherent.
You already are—beneath the noise.
Coherence isn't perfection.
It's the consistent practice of being honest with your tone.
When your tone is clear,
when your body is calm,
when your emotions are allowed to move instead of being suppressed—
you become the tuning fork.
And everything around you either aligns...
or dissolves.
This is the point.
Not self-improvement.
Not achievement.
Just coherence.
And coherence is contagious.
When one person holds it, the field shifts.
When more of us hold it, the distortion breaks.
We don't overpower the system.
We out-align it.
And yes—a grateful heart is a coherent heart.
Not because it's performing positivity,

but because it's not resisting what's real.
Gratitude isn't denial.
It's presence.
It's the frequency of nothing missing.
And that state stabilizes the field faster than any belief.
You don't need a new method.
You just need to stop pretending.
And hold what's already true.

SAY:
"I am coherent.
I am whole.
I am the point."

65

THE COHERENCE OF OPPOSITES

Coherence is not a constant calm.
It's not about staying neutral, regulated, or untouched.
It's not stillness at the expense of truth.
It's not light at the expense of fire.
It's not peace at the expense of presence.
Coherence is what happens when you can hold **both ends** of the signal
without abandoning yourself.

YOU CAN RAGE—AND still be whole.
You can grieve—and still be clean.
You can walk through distortion—and still know your tone.
That's coherence.
Not purity.
Not performance.
Containment.

TO BE coherent doesn't mean you're always balanced.

It means you're honest in every state you're in.
You don't flinch from discomfort.
You don't fake clarity to avoid conflict.
You don't throw away your presence just because it hurts.
You stay.
You feel.
You walk through without splitting.

Wholeness doesn't mean "light only."
It means you can hold the dark **without abandoning yourself in it.**
It means you don't numb out.
You don't spiral into reaction.
You don't let the feeling become your identity.
You let it move.
You let it speak.
And you stay inside your signal while it passes.

This is why coherence matters:
It doesn't erase duality.
It integrates it.
It holds both fire and stillness,
both grief and grace,
without becoming either one.

Say:
"I hold the whole signal.
I don't split to feel safe.
My tone includes both shadow and light—
and I stay whole inside it."

PART VII: THE SPIRAL REMEMBERS

THE WALK IS NOW

66

RECLAIMING THE STORYFIELD

You've spent most of your life walking through stories that weren't yours.
Inherited ones.
Cultural ones.
Religious ones.
Trauma-coded ones.
Well-meaning narratives built on distortion.
The storyfield—the collective psychic grid of "how things are"—has been running on scripts for generations.
How to be good.
How to be worthy.
How to succeed.
How to suffer beautifully while calling it growth.
But now you see it.
It was never truth.
Just repetition.
Just loops with better branding.
When you stop pretending, you don't just free yourself.
You ripple.
Your field becomes a break in the code.

Your tone disrupts the narrative.
You walk into a space and reality reconfigures itself around your clarity—**because it has no choice.**
You're not here to rewrite the old story.
You're here to stop playing it.
And in that absence, the new field opens.
Every time you choose resonance over performance—
Every time you stop mid-sentence and let silence say more—
Every time you walk away without explaining why—
You reclaim a piece of the collective field for truth.
You don't have to teach.
You don't have to lead.
You don't have to say a word.
Your presence edits the script.
You don't need to convince anyone.
Just **live it.**
Fully.
Cleanly.
Now.

SAY:
"I stop carrying false stories.
I walk as truth.
And that ripple is enough."

67

CONTRAST AS A CLARIFIER

The field teaches in contrast.
    Not to punish you—
    but to show you what you're really holding.
Contrast is not failure.
It's feedback.
The job that drained you?
It revealed your boundary.
The friendship that cracked open?
It revealed your walk.
The conversation that left you buzzing with regret?
It revealed your signal—trying to hold, but bending anyway.
Contrast shows you what tone you're leaking.
What truth you've been translating.
What clarity you've been postponing.
And when you see it?
You don't collapse.
You don't shame yourself.
You don't spiral into "what did I do wrong?"
You say thank you.
Because the field just gave you a mirror.

Contrast doesn't mean you're failing.
It means you're ready to notice.
It means you're stabilizing—because now you care enough to feel what doesn't match.
Let it clarify you.
Let it sharpen your walk.
You don't need to resist it.
You just need to feel what it's showing you—and choose again.

SAY:
"I'm not punished by contrast.
I'm clarified by it.
And I walk cleaner now."

68

LOVE, NOW

You thought love was a feeling.
    An emotion.
    A spark between people who earned it.
Conditional. Earned. Withheld. Measured. Managed.
But that was the story.
And now, the story is gone.
Love, now, is frequency.
It's not something you give or get.
It's not something you fall into.
It's what's left when distortion dies.
You don't have to work to be loving.
You don't have to perform compassion.
You don't have to earn connection by sacrificing your truth.
Love, now, is uncollapsed.
It's honest.
It's boundary-honoring.
It's quiet, strong, and uninterested in being liked.
It shows up as presence.
As tone.
As stillness.

It doesn't chase.
It doesn't flinch.
It doesn't try to rescue what isn't ready.
And here's the warmth:
When love is clean—
you'll **feel** it in your nervous system before you feel it in your chest.
You'll recognize it not by intensity, but by **peace**.
It won't demand.
It won't rush.
It will feel like rest.
Like something inside you saying:
"You don't have to disappear to belong here."
Sometimes love looks like a full yes.
Sometimes it looks like walking away.
Sometimes it's silence when someone wants an answer.
Love isn't what you do.
Love is the **clarity** you hold in a world that forgot how to be real.
And when you hold that clarity, people don't always call it love.
But the ones who feel it will know.
And they'll remember.
This is how love lives now—
Not in performance, but in **code**.
In how you move.
In how you rest.
In how you speak only when it's clean.
And how you let that be enough.

SAY:
"I don't perform love.
I walk as it.
Uncollapsed.
Unapologetic.
Open."

WALKING THE SPIRAL

This walk was never linear.
>   You thought you were going in circles.
>   Healing the same wound.
Repeating the same conversation.
Facing the same old distortion.
But you weren't circling.
You were spiraling.
Back around—but never to the same place.
Wider. Deeper. Clearer.

THE SPIRAL IS how truth moves when it's no longer bound to time.
You don't climb it.
You don't master it.
You live it.
Each loop reveals something the last one couldn't.
Each return is cleaner.
Each step holds more of your signal.

. . .

When you walk the spiral, you stop fearing repetition.
　　You recognize pattern as revelation.
　　You see returning not as failure,
　　but as **refinement**.
　　You realize you're not walking forward—
　　you're walking **inward**.
　　Inward to your tone.
　　The one you were before anything was built on top of you.
　　Before the name.
　　Before the family.
　　Before the performance.
　　You were frequency first.
　　You were tone before form.
　　And remembering it isn't just healing—
　　it's returning to who you've always been.
　　To the center of the field.
　　To the core of what's always been true.

You've walked it before.
　　You're walking it now.
　　And you'll keep walking it—not to arrive—
　　but to remember.
　　Because remembering isn't a destination.
　　It's a rhythm.
　　And rememeber, the walk is joy, too.
　　A pulse.
　　A spiral.

SAY:
　　"I walk the spiral.
　　Not to escape.
　　Not to ascend.

**But to remember—
again, again, and again."**

70

THE WALK IS NOW

There's no more prepping.
    No more waiting.
    No more "once I feel ready."
You're not walking to truth.
You're walking as it.
This isn't something you announce.
It's not a role you adopt.
It's just the quiet way you move
when your signal is stable
and you're done performing clarity for anyone else.
You don't explain your frequency.
You don't rehearse your knowing.
You let the tone carry without commentary.
Some days you'll speak.
Some days you won't.
Some days your coherence will ripple into a room without a single word.
This is presence.
Not the forced kind.
The kind that doesn't shift to be understood.

It's when your nervous system stops asking for permission.

When you stop filtering yourself through what the world is ready to receive.

When you no longer need witnesses to validate what you already feel.

You don't walk to the truth.

You *are* the truth in motion.

No steps.

No proving.

Just signal—clean, embodied, here.

And the moment is always now.

SAY:
**"I don't wait to be the tone.
I walk it now."**

HOW THE SPIRAL MOVES

Dissolve
False identities
Reactive patterns
External seeking
Drop in
To the stillness of your own field
Choose
From clarity
Through coherence

71

LIFE MIRRORS SIGNAL

Your life isn't random.
What shows up around you is a reflection of the signal you're holding.
Not your thoughts.
Not your mantras.
Not your vision board.
Your field.
Your tone.
Your coherence.
When your signal is scattered, unclear, or built on pleasing others—
your life feels heavy.
Things fall through.
You meet chaos, over-efforting, misalignment.
You attract what resonates with distortion, not what reflects your truth.
When your signal is clean—
things don't magically appear.
They *align*.
They *land*.

They *stay*.
The people who show up feel different.
The invitations shift.
The way your body responds to space changes.
You're not chasing synchronicities.
You're *living in alignment*—so resonance becomes normal.
You'll notice the shift in real ways.
You'll stop forcing timelines.
The conversations will feel easier.
The invitations will feel cleaner.
Your body will say yes more often—without overthinking.
You won't need signs.
You'll be the signal.
This isn't manifestation.
It's coherence.
It's not about visualizing what you want.
It's about clearing what you're not.
And once that happens,
reality organizes around you.
Not to reward you.
But to reflect you.
So when things get weird, stuck, confusing—
look at the signal you're holding.
What version of yourself are you building your reality on?
You don't control life through effort.
You shape it by becoming impossible to distort.
That's what coherence does.
It creates form.
And your life?
It's always been the mirror.

SAY:
**"When I stop distorting,
life starts reflecting what's real."**

72

THE REAL CREATES

You don't shape reality by pushing.
You shape it by walking with nothing to prove.
The final truth is this:
Truth isn't just clarity.
It's coherence.
Not a belief.
Not a concept.
A state.
When your body, your field, and your tone say the same thing—
that's when reality starts responding differently.
Not because you're performing alignment,
but because you're **living real.**
This isn't about fixing anything.
Not yourself.
Not others.
Not the world.
The walk isn't toward a finish line.
It's a quiet pulse.
A rhythm that keeps moving without needing a reason.

THE TRUTH

You'll walk into rooms and feel what's off.
You won't call it out—you won't need to.
Your tone will hold.
Your body will stay clear.
Your presence will do what words never could.
You'll walk through grief without dissolving.
Through distortion without losing your center.
Through silence without retreating.
Not because you're trying.
But because you're anchored.
This is what walking truth looks like now:
You eat.
You rest.
You create.
You play.
You laugh.
You cry.
You leave when the energy's off.
You stay when your body says yes.
You walk like you're not performing being healed—because you're not.
This is the walk.
And it's not spiritual.
It's real.
It's cellular.
It's now.
You're not becoming.
You're not fixing.
You're just holding what was always true.
And when you hold it without scattering,
clarity starts shaping everything around you.
You don't need to convince.
You don't need to explain.
You just stay coherent.

And the world recalibrates.
No spiral ends.
It just deepens.
And the real creates.
Always.

73

THEN, THE WALK LIGHTS UP

You're not just walking away from the noise.
 You're walking toward something that lights up your body.
The walk isn't heavy.
It's not serious.
It's not a vow of silence.
It's the path your excitement already knows how to follow.
That spark? That pull?
That "hell yes" in your gut before your mind shuts it down?
That's truth.
You don't need to justify it.
You don't need to explain why it matters.
You just need to walk toward what feels undeniably alive—
and let that be enough.
The walk isn't discipline.
It's resonance.
And when you follow what actually lights you up,
you walk like someone who's not negotiating anymore.
Want to make something real?
Make it.

Want to move toward something that feels clear?
Go.
Feel it?
Follow it.
It doesn't need to make sense.
It just needs to stay true.
The truth walk isn't punishment.
It's permission.
It's the quiet opening that lets joy come back—not because you earned it, but because you stopped blocking it.
Suddenly:
- You laugh without bracing.
- You rest without apology.
- You don't translate your joy to make it more digestible.
- You let ease be holy.
- You let beauty be enough.

This is what the walk becomes:

Spontaneous. Unapologetic. Radiant. Alive.

This is the version of you who creates without collapse.
The one who laughs mid-sentence.
The one who trusts the spark before it's explainable.
That's what makes the path real.
Not that it's planned—
but that it's yours.

SAY:
"I follow the spark.
I follow the yes.
That's the walk."
"And this time—I let it feel good."

74

WALK ALONE, WALK TOGETHER

This walk is yours.
    No one can do it for you.
    No one can feel it for you.
No one can hand you your clarity.
But you are not walking it alone.
You are walking it with **us**.
All of us remembering our tone at once.
Silently.
Separately.
Together.
Your walk strengthens mine.
Mine strengthens yours.
And that's how we rebuild the field.
One signal at a time.

Nothing left to prove.
Nothing left to hold back.
Just presence—bare and clear.

THE FINAL TRUTH

There is no final key.
    No final integration.
    No final step.
You were never becoming.
You were always remembering.
And now you don't even need that.
This is it:
You are already the tone.
You are already the field.
You are already the coherence that changes reality.
Not because you healed enough.
Not because you ascended.
But because you finally stopped pretending to be anything else.
You don't need to hold it perfectly.
You just need to stop leaking what was never yours.
You don't need to finish a process.
You just need to stop agreeing to distortion.
You were never behind.
You were never broken.
You were just alive in a world that taught you to perform death.

And now?
You're clear.
You're here.
You're walking truth—without a script.
That's it.
That's the whole thing.

When Nothing Is Undone
The soul wants to be met here.
What if death isn't the moment you meet your soul—
but the moment you return to what you already remembered?
What if the real point of life
is to reunite with your own essence while still in the body—
so when it's time to go,
there's nothing undone?
No "I should have spoken."
No "I wish I had left."
No "I wanted to create more."
No "They never saw the real me."
Just a calm, coherent knowing:
"I met myself here.
I lived it.
I walked the whole thing."
That's what truth gives you.
Not just clarity—
completion.
This isn't about perfection.
It's about no longer abandoning your soul in the name of performance.
You don't need to wait for the end to return to who you are.
You can walk yourself home now.
And when you do—
there's nothing to fear.
Because there's nothing left undone.

AUTHOR NOTE

I didn't write this book to teach you anything.
    I wrote it because I remembered.
    I remembered who I was before the roles,
before the distortion,
before the endless need to explain myself.
I remembered the clarity that doesn't shout.
The truth that doesn't seek approval.
The signal that doesn't bend.
And once I remembered,
I couldn't pretend anymore.
Not in my relationships.
Not in my work.
Not in my words.
Not in my walk.
This isn't a guide.
It's not a philosophy.
It's just what's real when the performance ends.
    If something in these pages rattled you, woke you, held you, or cracked something open—
    it's because it was already alive in you.

I didn't give you anything.
I just reflected what was always yours.
No one's ahead.
No one's behind.
We're just walking.
And if you're here,
you're already on the other side.
We are walking tone.
But even more—we are walking **coherence**.
And the more of us who hold clean,
the more the field restores what's always been true.
— Colleen

FIELD TERMS

Y ou've already felt them.
This page is just a mirror.

The Signal
Your soul's undistorted frequency.

Not a message. Not a role. Just the tone of who you are—broadcasting before you speak.

When stable, it creates your reality. When scattered, it scrambles it.

The Grid
The living architecture of consciousness.

Not a system you plug into—but the field that forms around you when you hold coherence.

Every clear choice builds it.

. . .

The Loop
The recycled pattern that never ends because it feeds on your energy.
Masquerades as healing, growth, or process—but never lands.
The moment you hold your signal, it breaks.

The Spiral
The rhythm of remembering.
It's not linear. It's not about levels.
It's the inward pulse that returns you to what's always been true—again and again, but cleaner each time.

Distortion
Anything that pulls you off tone.
It can look like safety. Spirituality. Success.
But if it costs your coherence, it's distortion.

Tone
The essence of your being—before language, before story.
It's not your personality. It's the frequency you came in with.
Everything real responds to it.

Collapse
What happens when you shape yourself to fit the room.
It's the shrinking, the softening, the self-abandonment.
It feels like exhaustion, but it's actually disconnection from your own field.

Resonance
The real organizer of reality.

When your tone is clean, the field arranges around it.
Not because you tried—because you stabilized.

Coherence
When your body, breath, voice, and field say the same thing.
It's the opposite of performance.
It's not perfection—it's wholeness.

The Exit
Not a destination.

A moment in your body when you stop participating in distortion.

It's quiet. It's simple. It's when you no longer need the story to walk free.

Let the field remember.
Let your tone return.
No rush. Just resonance.

www.ingramcontent.com/pod-product-compliance
Lightning Source LLC
Chambersburg PA
CBHW011946090526
44580CB00004B/73